On a clear day you can see Barnsley Town Hall

Attitudes to our Environment

Edited by
Ian Clayton

Everyone has a story to tell. We find ways of helping them tell it.

YORKSHIRE ART CIRCUS

Published by Yorkshire Art Circus,
School Lane, Glasshoughton,
Castleford, West Yorkshire, WF10 4QH
Telephone 0977 550401

Typesetting by Print Assist, Castleford

Printed by FM Repro Ltd., Repro House, 69 Lumb Lane,
Roberttown, Liversedge

Additional photographs – William Hollins, Stephen McClarence,
Volker Bredebusch

ISBN 0 947780 56 4

Yorkshire Art Circus is a unique book publisher. We link our books with performances and exhibitions and offer workshops for the first time writer.
Yorkshire Art Circus projects have successfully toured community centres, colleges, galleries, clubs, galas and art centres. In all our work we bring new artists to new audiences.

For details of our programme of performances, exhibitions, conferences and workshops send for our brochure and book list at the address above.

Yorkshire Art Circus is a non-profitmaking limited company.

Yorkshire Art Circus would like to thank the libraries at Barnsley, Grimethorpe, Cudworth and Royston, also Penistone History Group and Grimethorpe Neighbourhood Centre, Margate Street for their part in this project.

We would like to thank the following people who have contributed to this book:

Margaret McFarlane
Betty Robinson
Jack Jubb
Phyllis Crossland
Mary Watson
Betty Armstrong
Linda Finny
Tony Thomson
Tony Clayton
Linda Rogers
Marjorie Rogerson
Margaret Ogley
Harold Wright
Stan Hardy
Vera Bough
Jack Booty
Kathleen Miles
Ruth Cockburn
Pauline Hirst
Joan Cartwright
Joan Machen
Madelaine Butterfield
Dot Doughty
Janet Eaglesfield
Brian Lewis
Harry Malkin
Muriel Hobson
Jack Townsend
Harold Graham
Helen Bodnar
Katherine Denby
Angela Jennison
Monica Wignall
Margaret Marsh
Dick Brownhill
Vera Nicholson
Lucy Hanwell
Pauline Moffitt
Jack Booty
Angie Round
Rachel Adam
Hilda Clark
John Hudston
Albert Smith
Constance Middlethwaite
Edna Hardy
Ralph Hibbert
Joan Franks
Jean Schorah
Ruth Leadbeater
Ray Hearne
Myrna Parry
June Winstanley
Phil Paver
Tom Doughty
John Foxton
Linda McGillivray
Mick O'Connor
Ernest Cooper
Evelyn Dabbs
Fred Minnis
Ken Hirst
Stephen McClarence
Gillian Walker
Lillian Moorhouse
John Smethurst
Jean Bloodworth
Fred Minnis
Joan Kenworthy
Alan Armstrong
Jack Wassell
Janet Ingram
Ethel Watson
Joseph Eels
Bill Hunt
Mick Wilson
Doris Howarth
Arthur Stringer
Cynthia Rooke
Joyce Davy
Catherine Silverwood
Edith Haslehurst
Joan Monk
Dorothy Hague
Ellen Hargate
Ian Clayton
Margaret Edwards
Terry Haggerty
Christine Moorby
Audrey Haggerty
Liz Hall
Mary Watson
Jack Peach
Peter Morgan
Pam Yates
Ruth Vyse

Editorial Back Up Team

Margaret Milner
Hilary Brooke
Reini Schühle
Brian Lewis
Olive Fowler
John Foxton
Stuart Hawkes
Cheron Stevenson
Lynda Finney
Tony Lumb
Rachel Van Riel

Steve McClarence

Robin Hood and his Merry Men

Supported by:

YORKSHIRE ARTS

BARNSLEY LIBRARIES

BARNSLEY Metropolitan Borough Council

CONTENTS

INTRODUCTION

This book gets its title from a remark made by one of the contributors, during a walk in the rhododendron woods on the ridge that overlooks Grimethorpe.

We decided to start our environmental book project in Grimethorpe because, despite the pollution in and around the village, there is great beauty within walking distance. We were also impressed by the people's knowledge of their environment, their appreciation for the countryside and their resolution in the face of an increasingly polluted world.

We found this to be true as we moved the project on through Cudworth, Shafton, into Barnsley itself and then out as far as Penistone.

There is much more awareness of the environment these days and if the anecdotes in this book, both past and present, are anything to go by, folk round Barnsley way are in the vanguard of the cleaner future movement.

WHERE THERE'S MUCK . . . .

The word of the sanitary inspector was law

□ If you climb up onto the hills all round Barnsley you can get grand views of the town itself and on a clear day you can see the Town Hall, shining out in the sun. I've seen it from up Brierley Common and as you come down the hill towards Grimethorpe and Cudworth you can see right over onto the Pennines. They tell me you can see Barnsley from as far away as Penistone. You can definitely see it from the limestone ridge at the back of Doncaster. That's on a clear day, of course, and it's true to say that we get our fair share of smoggy ones, but at the end of the day it's people that matter most. The folk round here are lovely and that's what outsiders can't weigh up when they talk about Barnsley being a mucky hole. We might not have much brass but we're happy.

□ There was a woman in Grimethorpe who was known to everybody. She was, well, the only way to put it is to say she was a legend, one never to be forgotten. She was the complete all rounder. There was absolutely nothing she couldn't do, she used to be up with the larks and go round to them that were on days and knock them up. She had a long prop which she used to reach the upstairs window. She was up before half past four every morning and got paid a tanner for it. Then she went on errands for people at a rate of a penny a time. Endless times she would go on errands in a day, as like as not to the pawn shop. She threw coal in for the miners when their allowance came and got a few buckets for herself for that and she used to buy things from the Co-op and allow people to tick off her. Many is the time she was taken down by allowing people to borrow. I used to ask her why she let people have food and cigs and buckets of coal when in a lot of cases there wasn't much chance of getting it back. All she did was laugh and say she didn't mind helping folk. She was a big rawboned woman and stood 6 foot 3 inches but she was gentle and caring and I'm sure everybody liked her. The only job she didn't do was look after kids. They were mostly timid of her, possibly due to her habit of putting her hand inside her blouse and saying "Come on here and I'll give you some tit," but as they got older they got used to her.

□ Florrie Bailey, now there was a woman. I can't say enough good things about her. Whenever you saw her she'd be swaggering down with a shovel over her shoulder and by hell she could scoff some work. She had a bamboo cane with some wires stuck in the end which she used to wake people up. If she couldn't hear any stirring she'd shout up, "Right, I've been once this is the last time."

□ You used to get fed up of getting up at that time in a morning to find out that there was no work to go to. Of course, no work meant no money, then you went short of food and the vicious circle that poverty brings round really began. Poor living conditions, little or no recreation and relaxation and poor health. It seemed at one point that just as one epidemic ended another one began. My father never saw the pit for two months. He was a main bearer at funerals and during one of the diphtheria epidemics it seemed as though he was out every day taking some poor bugger down to the cemetery.

□ During the early part of 1928 there were a number of cases of scarlet fever. In those days it was treated as a very serious illness and my sister and I developed it at the same time. My mother told our symptoms to the family doctor, a Dr Walsh, and he said it sounded like measles and that he would call round. I remember it as though it was yesterday. He ran his finger down my sister's chest and just said, "It's scarlet." No need to mention fever. We were ordered to bed and told to stay there. Mother had to dip a sheet in disinfectant and hang it outside he bedroom door. Father was told that on no account must he come to see us as he would be mixing with other men at work who could carry the germ home with them. I can't say we were really ill, just a sore throat and covered from head to toes in a vivid red rash but we were worried that we might be sent away to Kendray Hospital. We were still in bed a fortnight later and felt sure we would not be taken away when suddenly all our hopes were shattered when one afternoon the peace was broken by a loud slamming of doors. I rushed to the bedroom window and saw an ambulance and a nurse walking to our house with a blanket over her arm. We learnt afterwards that two boys who lived not far away had been taken into hospital the day before.

How strange everything looked as we were taken into the long ward full of other children, some very ill and some on the mend. Things in that hospital were pretty much as they are today, tests made and temperatures taken every now and then. After two weeks we seemed to be getting much better and we were moved to Lundwood Fever Hospital where we met other children who we knew. At this point we both developed kidney trouble as a side effect of the fever and were put into a side ward where they piled six blankets and four water bottles into each of our beds. This caused us to breed lice in our heads and we had to wear what was commonly known as a saffron cap, usually associated with children who had dirty hair. My mother and father were only

Grimethorpe Wedding

allowed to speak to us through the windows and were horrified at what had happened. They would have been even more horrified if they had heard the matron say on one of her visits, "Who's got the filthy head?" That was the worst thing anyone had ever said to us.

We seemed to be in that hospital for an eternity and it gave us plenty of time to reflect on how we came about our illness in the first place. Mother said the germ came from the Alhambra Theatre. It was our family custom to have a treat every time we got the Co-op dividend. We would go to a lovely cafe on Doncaster Road in Barnsley and have a toasted teacake and a chocolate eclair apiece. I remember as kids we were fascinated by the dumb waiter in that cafe. Then after the cafe we would go to the Alhambra.

When the news came that we were to go home we were given a thorough checking over to see if all the loose scales on our hands and feet had gone. We finally passed and went home on a glorious sunny Easter Saturday. I was still unable to go to school for a further three weeks and all my school books had to be burned. That was one of the saddest things but Mr Bennet the sanitary inspector said that it had to be, so there was no argument about it. In those days the word of the sanitary inspector was law.

□ The sanitary inspector was a man spoken about in hushed tones, a man on a pedestal high above us lesser mortals. His name always came in inverted commas. The mere uttering of the threat "I'll set the sanitary inspector on you" was enough to send shivers down the spine. Nowadays when you go to the council to try and get something done it's "Oh you mean you'd like to see the Environmental Health Officer." Then you have to go through all the rigmarole and departments and you're no wiser when you come out. You can't threaten anybody with the sanitary

Union Officials — 1940's

inspector these days because they all know he doesn't exist, and even if he does he is lost in the maze of corridors and offices that make up the palace of bureaucracy that they call the Town Hall.

□ We used to live in the middle of nowhere at Sidlow's Farm so whenever we wanted a doctor we couldn't get one. Them at Houghton said that we lived in Grimethorpe and vice-versa. When it came that I was pregnant, my dad said, "We will bloody find out where we live once and for all" and he did. That's how we came to know that we lived in Grimethorpe.

□ A lovely young woman and a right old man came to lodge with us at the farm. I think they were supposed to be wed. Mother said we weren't to bother the young woman because she wasn't well. We knew she was pregnant. Some time after she gave birth but it caused a lot of distress. The baby died almost straight away but I pestered my mother so much to see it that eventually she let me go into the bedroom and look. They had laid the baby on the window-sill wrapped up. It didn't half look a picture. The mother, poor lass, was in a terrible state and she died soon after. I've thought about it over the years and realised as I've got older that there must have been some horrible disease in the house.

Shortly after the deaths the Health Authority came and told us to bury all the bedding. I remember mother was very angry because the blankets were nearly new woollen ones. We had to bury all the clothes as well. I don't know what disease it was, for there were a lot of them about then. People were kept in ignorance by the health authorities. I don't suppose much changes, though. We're kept in the dark today about what's put in the food so it's just the same.

□ I never trained as a midwife but like a

lot of women I used to help out where I could. The first time I helped with a birth was one Friday morning. I'd been blackleading and I didn't even have time to wash my hands. The mother of one of the babies I'd helped with came back for me a few weeks after and said the baby was badly. I went to have a look. I've never seen anything like it, the poor kid was laid in the corner looking like death warmed up and with a terrible cough. The father and his cronies were sat at the table drunk, carding and smoking, ignoring the baby and its mother. That's no kind of environment to bring a kid up in.

□ My father stopped carding after he said he heard the devil rattling his chains in the corner at home. They always say that when you've got cards in the house you've got the devil in.

□ I once went to mend the electric at a house and said to the woman that it was only the fuse that was missing from the main switch. "Ssssh!" she said, "it's t'only way I can stop his carding."

□ We didn't even have a chemist in Grimethorpe at one time. If you wanted anything like that you'd walk to Cudworth. Most folk used to go across to see Dr Thompson, he had three colours of medicine; red, dark brown and black. The red one – some called it his cherry or raspberry medicine – was lovely. Kids used to drink it as pop, they couldn't afford pop anyway. The black one was for colds and had liquorice and chlorodine in it.

□ We had plenty of good local remedies. If anybody had whooping cough or bad sinuses they used to take them down to where they were gas tarring the roads and say "Have a good smell at that." Up Cudworth way there was a stream that ran under a tunnel known as the monkey tunnel. The water was freezing cold there and ideal for them that

had sprained ankles or bruised legs. Of course for anything serious they'd send you away; people who had TB had to go to a sanatorium at Ilkley.

□ There seemed to be a lot more funerals in years gone by, folk dying all the time. I suppose there were more illnesses and diseases knocking about then. A good funeral was an entertainment for a lot of folk, though, they used to like standing to watch the procession. There was a tradition that the horsemen and pall-bearers got a gallon of ale. Then they'd pass round the chocolate finger biscuits.

□ I'm a great believer in old-fashioned cures for most ailments. It's easy for doctors these days to prescribe pills for everything. There must be half the population of this country addicted to tranquilisers or sleeping tablets. Comfrey is a marvellous herb for anything from calming you down to rheumatism and sprains. Marigold tea will bring spots out; for things like measles the quicker the rash breaks out the better. And you can't beat brown sugar and onion or garlic for colds and asthma. Leave it to stand in a saucer overnight, it's just like 'liquafruta'. For sleeplessness they say the outer leaves of a lettuce made into a tea is good but I'm a good sleeper so I wouldn't know.

□ When I had earache my dad used to blow the smoke from his pipe down my ear, it worked every time. When you had a sore throat they used to put a bit of sulphur on some paper and blow it down your throat. When kids peed the bed they used to make them a mouse pie.

□ They used to stop a tanner a week at the pit for treatment at Dr Thompson's and there was a Nursing Association. Somebody collected threepence a week door-to-door for that and at the end of the year they had a big dinner do. The Co-op had a scheme as well, where if you got so

Captain Addy's House

"See how bad it is"

many recommends you could go to hospital. It ran a convalescent home at Mablethorpe as well. The Club and Institute Union had homes at Pegwell Bay in Kent and Morecambe.

□ Captain Addy who owned the pit was a very shy man and frightened to death of illnesses. One time when there was an epidemic going about he made every one of his staff gargle with salt water. Another time he had them all vaccinated with a needle, even the ones that didn't want it. He worried constantly about his own health and eating properly. There used to be more indigestion tablets on his table than snap.

□ The Captain used to send down for an electrician when he wanted a bulb changing. He even had an electric plate warmer back in the 1930s.

□ You can come down that hill where Captain Addy lived and see how bad Grimey is for your health. See the air and how thick it is with pollution. It's shocking. And it drifts up over the school playground where kids are playing.

□ You don't need to work down the pit to get chest problems round here, you're exposed to muck from an early age. I suffer from bronchitis and living here is no good to me at all. Especially when it's damp and smoggy I have to go on breathing tablets. I always said I'd never marry a coal miner and I didn't but you're no better off, really, when you have to live among it.

You have to live somewhere though. We once moved to Skegness and worked at Butlins. I felt a lot better at the seaside but we ended up coming back to Grimethorpe. Folk used to say, "Ooh dear! Whatever have you come back here for?" but what can you do? Your family are here, folk are friendly and you need your roots if nothing else.

Cudworth Railway Accident

□ My dad was born in Grimethorpe, suffered with his health through the pit here and he'll die here. We keep trying to encourage him to move but he won't now, he's too set in his ways, and he claims he'll die a lot quicker in the open world.

□ They talk about privatising the pits. I'll tell you a story about the heartache of private enterprise. My brother fell down the shaft at Grimethorpe Pit and was killed after getting into the sump at the bottom. I'll never forget the look on my mother's face when we broke the news. She had the strength of two men when we tried to restrain her from going to the pit yard. The pit officials wouldn't let us know anything and the authorities were even worse at the inquest. We got to know nothing apart from a verdict of death by misadventure. The compensation came...£500, plus a bit from the union. Is that what a man's life is worth? The money was put in trust for his children and the wife had to apply to the court everytime she wanted to buy new Whitsun clothes.

Another relative of ours had his neck broken at the pit and died. They wheeled his body home on a handcart, with his head hanging over the side. His poor mother had to wash him and lay him out. Don't talk to me about private enterprise!

□ An old man who lived near me had to pack work in. They said he had bronchitis, then later on they said it was tuberculosis but he finally died of pneumoconiosis. His wife was in a complete turmoil, she didn't know who to believe, who to trust. I went with her to collect the death certificate and there it was in black and white *pneumoconiosis*. It's a crying shame when they won't tell you anything.

□ A lot die from emphysema, the great unrecognised miners' disease. An American scientist has proved that your chances of getting it if you are a miner are twenty times more than if you are another worker. The trouble is that you can also get it from smoking so the government choose not to classify it as an industrial disease. Of course the Coal Board couldn't give a bugger and the Union links it so closely with bronchitis that they haven't got a chance in hell of getting it recognised as an industrial disease.

□ There were some terrible smogs in Cudworth, what with the pits and water vapour and steam trains at the railway station. A lot of people won't know it but Cudworth was the biggest open air railway station in this country. A lot of people walked about with a scarf across their mouths and when they took it off you could see a big black mark on it.

□ It was exciting watching the trains down at Cudworth Station, eight platforms there was. *The Devonian* used to go to Bournemouth and Torquay and all them lovely seaside places. You could set your watch by it, ten to six every night.

□ In the days of the London to Liverpool Railway an old man had a three sided poultry pen next to the main line using the banking as the fourth side. Of course the hens could run up the banking quite easily and consequently were killed by passing trains. So the old man, in an effort to stop this happening, went to the railway station to buy a timetable to hang in the 'hen 'oil'. But alas he had to admit this had done no good, as he said ruefully, "The damned trains never run on time." That was over Penistone way.

□ Another tale they attribute to Penistone was the one during the wartime blackout about old Alf working on nights. He was walking in total darkness on a lonely road to his place of employment. The wind was blowing in Alf's face and his efforts to light his clay pipe were proving useless. So he turned round, back to the wind, and lit his pipe. He then forgot to turn round again and walked all the way back home.

A marble fireplace in the garage

□ They really pulled a flanker on us with this smokeless fuel business. The NCB gave a grant about seven years ago for people to switch to central heating with a back boiler system. People continued to burn coal though or mix coal and coke together. Then we were told we had to go smokeless, it cost us a fortune. We couldn't get a grant this time because they said our grates were already designed for smokeless fuel but they were no good, so we had to change again at our own expense. I paid nearly a thousand pounds for my new fireplace. The stupid thing is that the Coalite plant and the power station are still pumping out their fumes so I can't see as how we are any better off.

□ My dad bought his house off the pit when they were trying to get everybody to buy them. He had it all remodernised and put a beautiful marble fireplace in. A few months after the council came and said that the area was going smokeless and that he would have to put in a Parkray burner. He kicked up a real fuss against it but it did no good. Now he's stuck with a two hundred pound marble fireplace in his garage.

□ I went into somebody's house the other day, they'd bought a brand new marble effect fireplace. They've had gas central heating for years so they'd no need for it. The fire hole itself was full of dried flowers; everybody commented on how nice it looked. I'm not so sure, fireplaces are better with coal in instead of dry flowers.

□ What's the point in making a coal mining town smokeless, every bugger round here smokes anyway. Ill health is one of the hazards of mining and you expect it to come.

I'd like to see the air monitored by some kind of independent body. When you ask they always tell you it's clean or there's nothing harmful in it but clean compared to what? Who sets the standard? Is there a standard to start with? All I know is that because my windows face the Coalite plant and because of the prevailing west winds I have to wash my windows and my sills every two or three days. They tell you that it's safe but something that causes black smoke and smells as bad as that does can't be healthy, can it?

□ We don't get any compensation for the muck in the air round here and it stinks sometimes. When you ask about it they tell you that it's *sulphurous*. I don't know about that, it smells like pure shit to me.

□ Another thing about this smokeless business is that it has caused a lot of people to do away with open fires all together. Well, that means of course that there's a lot more rubbish about than before because folk aren't burning it. Then the dogs come and tip the bins over and you've got a problem with the smell and litter blowing about everywhere. It makes you wonder what's worse, pollution from smoke in the air like we've always had, or rotten rubbish in the streets.

□ There used to be some bad smells in the air round here at one time. When they did their own slaughtering, they did it in the back yards where they kept the pigs. It used to stink in summer; boiling offal and skin and bones. All the kids used to line up and watch. Then there was the night soil, by hell there was some pong from that. It's a wonder we didn't have fever as kids. We used to go down near the pit yard and look where the midden men had thrown it. One of our mates fell in once, up to his eyeballs in it he was, we had to pull him out and carry him home in a wheelbarrow.

Main Gate Rippers

Queen Street Backs

□ I would say that traffic causes the greatest amount of air pollution in Grimethorpe these days, especially the lorries that are running up and down from the pit all the time. We normally get thirty or forty an hour going past but I once counted fifteen in a quarter of an hour. It looks terrible up Engine Lane with them, the grass verges on both sides of the road are as black as coal. Not even weeds, never mind wild flowers, would grow there.

□ My uncle, who had lived in an industrial part of Sheffield, said that the fresh air at the top of Hartcliff was better than the bracing air of Blackpool!

□ Years ago local farmers dug up the thistles and docks in their fields and rebuilt stone walls. Now that time means money to them so a spray of weed killer is supplemented, often without success, and posts and barbed wire have replaced the walls. A lot of vegetation, wild flowers and bird life in the district was lost some years ago when the local authority sprayed all the verges at the side of the roads. This has now been discontinued and the wildlife is returning.

□ I like to sleep with my window open but I still get up at pit time to close it as soon as the big lorries start. I counted three hundred one day starting at half past three in the morning. You can't sleep for them, what with the noise and the smell. When you've worked down the pit all your life and it comes to retiring you shouldn't have to put up with that. They don't cover the lorries and they're supposed to and there was an agreement between the council and the coal board about routing through the village but they don't stick to it. It's like everything else, if it's not on their own doorstep folk don't want to know and the lorry drivers themselves aren't bothered because they're on bonus and making their money.

Cudworth Orphan Procession

☐ For the number of local people that Coalite plant and power station employs it's not worth all the hassle. You tend to find in an area like this where they've destroyed a lot of the natural beauty and replaced it with pollution and filth in the streets, that they justify it by saying that it's good for the local economy and provides some necessary work. Well, in my opinion that argument is no longer applicable to Grimethorpe. As far as I'm concerned they can take their pollution and stick it up their own back yard!

☐ The scourge of all coal miners is dust. Call it what you like – pneumoconiosis, silicosis, black lung disease – they're all the same. It's not the coal that causes it, it's the rock dust and you can work next to a man all your life and you won't get it but he will. You don't have to work underground to get a chest infection. I've known people who've never worked in the pit go to see the specialists in Sheffield. When they realise that they're from Grimey it's as though they say, "Oh no, not another!"

☐ I think people were a lot fitter in years gone by due to them working a lot harder, both the women in the home and the men at the pit. You didn't see so many overweight people then like you do these days. Same with the children, running back and forwards to the shops all the time. Now shopping is done once for the whole week. It's freezers, fridges, more money, less work and unhealthy people.

☐ They talk about the poverty in the 1930s, yes, that's true, but the poverty of women at that time was real poverty. My mother like a lot of other folks' mothers round here was a very weak and sickly looking woman for a lot of her life, bent up crooked and old long before her time. She used to be up at pit time then stop up, hard work all day and next to nowt to eat.

The kids and father were always fed first and she'd eat what was left. I can fair see her face now, standing with the door open at half past four in the morning listening for the buzzer that told the men whether they'd to go to work or not. Then when the buzzer went her face would turn an awful colour and everything would just flop. Men can talk about how rough they might have had it and how hard they had to work but there was more coal dug out at t'top boozer than at Grimethorpe pit. Don't let them kid you, the women suffered the poverty of those days far more than the men.

□ The undermanager at Frickley Colliery or one of them pits was a Mr. Smith, he was a pleasant man, one who understood the misery and hopelessness of the men seeking work. Even if he had no work to offer you, he did it with respect, and always wished you better luck in the search for work. You would go away without a job but you always had your dignity because he did not take that away, he gave it to you.

The undermanager at South Kirkby was as different again. He had no respect for anyone, not even those that were in work. His method was to treat you, yes, all of you, like dirt. He was a bully!

Pouring rules down our throats

□ As a small child I was confident that the air I breathed and the crystal clear tap water I drank were absolutely pure. Sadly today's children do not enjoy that same confidence in nature's basic provisions. The atmosphere is heavily polluted by power stations, industry, transport and domestic fossil fuel fires. Nitrates also drain off agricultural land which has been heavily treated with fertilizers and pesticides and finds its way into our water supplies.

Friends and colleagues called me a crank

Grimethorpe Pit Top

because of my views on pollution, whether it be of the atmosphere, water or food. I stopped eating beef when I learned that cattle were being given steroids to bulk them up. Some twenty years later most people are aware of the risk of high blood pressure and obesity from eating high quantities of beef and beef products. Even more disturbing is the incidence of spongiform encephalopathy, Mad Cow disease, which is now thought to be passed along the food chain causing similar symptoms in humans.

Once again nature was flaunted by farmers feeding livestock, which are herbivores, on dead animal meat and begging the question, do we really know what we are eating? I doubt very much if many of us do.

Atmospheric pollution worries me very much, the recent publicity about the Greenhouse Effect has made most people aware of the dangers of polluting the atmosphere. But are they aware of the insidious risk of severe illness or even early death from breathing in the invisible poisons in the air?

I became seriously interested in the subject of atmospheric pollution whilst employed as Nursing Officer for Health Visiting in the Pontefract Health District. In spite of excellent maternity and health visiting care given in the district the infant mortality rate was unacceptably high during the years 1976-1983 with the exception of 1982. In that year the rate fell to a record low of 17.5 deaths per thousand live births against the national rate of 11.5 for that year. I spent many hours considering the problem of infant mortality. I was convinced the babies were not dying because of poor ante-natal care or poor health visiting techniques, I knew that the standards of both these services in the area were excellent. I therefore felt sure the atmosphere in which expectant mothers and babies lived must have some connection with the deaths.

The sight of low flying aircraft twice a day has been a common feature in the

Banquet Al Fresco

Indoor Picnic

district for several years and I wondered whether the twice daily onslaught could be causing a down-draught or inversion of the low cloud which contained the emissions of smoke and sulphur dioxide from the power stations and other industries and from domestic fires. The problem worsened during the winter months which coincided with the majority of infant deaths.

I contacted an environmental health department and had a very helpful discussion with one of the officers there. The officer did not think that low flying aircraft could have any significant effect on the levels of air pollution. He did however make one interesting observation, he said of course the smoke and sulphur dioxide levels were much higher during the winter months, due to the increase in domestic fires, the smoke from the chimneys in cold damp weather did hang under a low cloud ceiling.

I decided to investigate the problem to see whether there was a connection between infant deaths and atmospheric pollution.

For a full year I spent every spare minute of my off duty time investigating the problem of atmospheric pollution in relation to infant deaths and still-births. I was allowed to visit other agencies during working hours to help with my study paper which I completed in 1983.

The findings were interesting and showed that while there was some relationship between sulphur dioxide and infant deaths there was a strong relationship between smoke and infant deaths.

I duly submitted my paper to my Senior Nursing Officers and to members of the working party who met monthly to discuss the problem of infant mortality in the district. To my dismay the paper was received and dismissed as not really relevant and too technical – a whole year's hard work was simply ignored.

"Pouring rules down our throats"

The infant death rate improved in the years from 1983 onwards and, interestingly, due to the valiant efforts of the environmental department the clean air programme was widened and the levels of smoke and sulphur dioxide also dropped. Could this be pure coincidence or was I correct in my assumption that there is a relationship between atmospheric pollution and infant mortality and still-birth?

Pollution levels have increased again in some areas especially one area where I have been told that people are burning fossil fuels in a designated clean air zone.

Will the infant mortality rate increase? Only time will tell.

☐ Is the answer to simply legislate, pour more rules and laws down throats to make people behave responsibly? That, surely, is only treating the symptoms and ignoring the causes. No amount of wrist-slapping is going to fundamentally alter our attitudes. It's a reassuring thought that some emphasis is being placed now in schools to educate the children towards a more environmentally aware perspective. The problem still remains, however, that once out of school, the pressures of a home environment that has the all day television seducing them with a multitude of superfluous stuff that parents feel blackmailed into having to afford – programmes that should insult even those with very limited intelligence – and a social system that tells them that the only way to get ahead is to earn lots of money, will combine to instil such fear of failure to achieve in these terms that even all of that will seem the easy option. What chance have they got when most adults are providing an example of ever increasing greed, arrogance, and material acquisitiveness? The modern family must have two cars, televisions in every room – with videos of course – new carpets, suites, latest model microwave and so on.

Strike 'em stiff

☐ We always got a lot of silverfish round here and crickets, especially when the tips were burning. Bed bugs were the worst, though. They used to stand the bed legs in cans of paraffin to stop them climbing up. When you bost them they smell terrible, you can smell them when they go past you on the pillow.

☐ There used to be an insect repellant called Strike 'Em Stiff. I was working in a house one day and there was a young lad eating a pan of hash, he complained to his mother that it was quite tasty but a bit hot. She said she'd only put a bit of pepper in, but when she come to look she'd put the Strike 'Em Stiff in.

☐ Electricians and the like hated working in what they called mucky houses and used to get 'bug money' on top of their ordinary wages. To claim it they had to hand in any bugs that they had found; they used to collect them in match boxes. One electrician told me that he was working in a house where there were two goats reared up on their back legs chewing at the wallpaper. When he asked the woman why she let the goats into the house she replied that it was much too cold for them outside.

☐ We'd been in the house a week or two when I first noticed the bed bugs. It nearly drove me out of my head. I had to get them shifted and went at it like a mad bull. I rubbed all round the house with sheep dip. I thought if it will get rid of sheep ticks it will get rid of 'owt but it didn't. It took ages before we eventually got shut. If we weren't in bed by nine o'clock they used to come down and fetch us. A lot of folk used to send round for Florrie and she'd come round with a kettle and pour boiling hot water on the bed springs.

☐ They say you can smell bed bugs, my sister went to my brother's new house with her nose in the air sniffing. Then announced "It's alright it only wants a good fettling, there's no bugs."

☐ They used to get what they called 'the itch', it was scabies really. They cured it by mixing flowers of sulphur and lard in a jar. We'd scrub ourselves every day, especially between the fingers.

☐ We had our own vet up White City. He wasn't the most hygienic of blokes. When folk used to take their dogs up for their tails docking he used to bite them off. 'Biting back' they called it.

☐ There's as many dogs as there are kids in Grimethorpe these days. Some of the gardens in the village area are full of dog muck and you can't expect kids to play in that, there's all sorts of diseases they can catch. There are a lot of Dobermans and Rottweilers, I think men round here like to buy them for their egos. A lot of people don't realise that big dogs like that take a lot of looking after, there's a lot of expense involved and apart from that there just isn't room for them to roam about round here.

☐ Disposable nappies are the bane of my life. A lot of people get on about dustbin men but do they realise what we have to put up with? Who wants to lift the lid off a bin and see a soiled nappy staring you in the face? There's some very mucky folk about I can tell you. Cat litters are another. I'm sick of getting grit stinking of cat pee down the back of my neck.

☐ I hope I live to see the day when it's compulsory for dogs to wear disposable nappies. You can't walk on the footpath for piles of dog muck. At the end of the hot summers when I was a girl you could sprawl across the warm pavement and draw in every clean square, and the mill girls coming home barefoot would teasingly swing their shoe heels close to your ears as they stepped over you. Not any more.

Steve McClarence

Over the garden wall

Steve McClarence

Make his day

□ There was a bloke used to walk his dog down near us and let it do its mess right outside our house. I wouldn't mind but he only lived at the top of the street. He didn't let his dog shit outside his own door, though. They've some cheek have some people. He carried on for ages, in the end my husband got browned off with it and went out to him. He said if he caught him fetching his dog down our end once more, he'd put the muck on a shovel, take it up to his own house and smear it all over his clean windows. He never came again.

□ Dog shit may not seem so important but if it is an indicator of attitudes to how we want to live then some of us are going to have huge problems coming to terms with the wider issues if we can't even get our act together on the basic and obvious ones.

□ I've seen a man take his dog for a walk and when it's done its 'doings' take a piece of toilet paper from his pocket, wipe its bottom and then throw the paper on the causeway.

□ You might be surprised to know that Cudworth is a nationally renowned centre of Pekinese dog breeding.

□ Our next door neighbour has got one of them Rottweilers. You ought to see it when it opens its mouth, it makes you shudder. I don't think they're a house dog. I said to the little lass that lives agin us, "Where do you keep your Zeus?" Apparently it's only allowed in the entrance. You can't treat a big dog like that.

A wedding cake shining in the sun

□ They say people are a product of their environment. When you look about round Grimethorpe, or any pit village for that

Steve McClarence

"Working together for a nice community"

matter, you can see that the miners with one or two exceptions are short well built fellows, well muscled and in a lot of cases with an aggressive demeanour. Can you imagine what folk are going to look like in a few years time, no jobs making everybody lazy, all these additives that are put into the snap and poisons getting into the water? They think that there's some rough looking buggers knocking about now, they've seen nothing yet!

□ If there was an international Big Belly competition some bugger in Grimey would win it.

□ Some people will work together for a nice community if they're encouraged. If one does it then others will follow. It's no trouble to keep your garden tidy, people aren't irresponsible when they're shown a better way. There's some lovely gardens amongst the dog muck round here. They've done a decent job regenerating the community up the top end of Darfield Road, the houses look all the same except they've painted the doors in different colours. They call it Rainbow Road now, they used to call it Giro City.

□ The landlords ought to take a lot more responsibility as regards the environment they've created. They don't seem to take any social responsibility whatsoever. Now that the so-called nuclear family has bought its own property which it jealously guards with neighbourhood watch schemes, what happens to those of us in rented accommodation? The 'problem' family as opposed to the 'nuclear' family is now welcomed with open arms by the landlords and do you know why? Because they get their rents paid directly, that's why. They don't have to worry now about going round collecting the overdue rents, in fact they don't even have to bother seeing the properties at all. It's a case of out of sight, out of mind.

Blackie & Pauline

□ One resident who complained about rats in her back yard was told that the housing repair allocation for cement had been spent on repair of elderly persons' footpaths; and that the broken drains encouraging the rats were the responsibility of the drains section but that poison was administered by the Environmental Health Department. This left the woman totally fed up and confused. As far as the council goes folk round here seem to be satisfied with them as landlords on the whole. It's just that they get frustrated at times by ivory towers in Barnsley.

□ There's one thing you can say, the atmosphere is much clearer these days. There used to be a time when you could barely see your hand in front of your face. Nowadays I can look out of my window and see Barnsley Town Hall; it's a big white building and stands there just like a great big tiered wedding cake shining in the sun.

□ I told my dad, a Midlander, that Barnsley Town Hall was built by the unemployed in the 1930s on a government scheme and that its tower was built of a specially compacted white cardboard. He believed me! On a clear day you can see Barnsley Town Hall from all over.

Grimethorpe – as pretty as a Christmas card

□ Sometimes when it's been snowing I like to walk up on the hill towards Brierley and look down across Grimethorpe. It's as pretty as a Christmas card. Then the snow melts and you see what industry has done to us. We're as entitled to a nice environment as anybody else....aren't we?

□ I wouldn't move out of Grimethorpe for a gold pig. I've got my family here and they're right friendly people. There might be one or two bad 'uns but you get that anywhere. Mind there's one or two

Steve McClarence

Margate Street Backs

Steve McClarence

"Entitled to a nice environment"

who've got a funny idea about snobbery. If you wash your net curtains too often they think you're stuck up so I generally take mine down and do them early in the morning. Same with the windows, I do them when it gets dark and they're all in watching television. It costs nowt to keep a clean house. At least the plumber dare put his head down the toilet when he comes.

□ They were strong in the miners' strike round here and now there's a lot of unemployment. You have only to look round to see that there's social deprivation but they don't have to tar everybody with the same brush. Some would have it that they're all thieves round here. I once sat on top of the coal bunker, as black as the fireback after getting a load in, when Scotch Alec the bobby come up and told me to empty it all back out again. He said I'd pinched it off the stacks. I hadn't, I'd paid for it but that's the sort of treatment we get.

□ I don't blame 'em for pinching a bit of coal to sell, in fact I encourage them. Anyhow it's not pinching, it's just sharing it out better.

□ The pit had a big ship's buzzer on top of the fanhouse. If it blew at half past eight at night you knew there was no work next morning. Sometimes you could go and there'd only be two hours work but you did it and got them to write it off. You could only get dole with three lieu days in, so if the pit reported two hours, you lost three days dole.

When they were sinking the shaft they built huts for the Irish sinkers to live in. When the sinkers moved out folk who couldn't afford to live anywhere else moved in. After the 1926 strike, a lot couldn't afford three shilling rent so they moved in, whole families living like navvies.

□ I think we used a lot more soap and

"A haze over the village"

water than they do now, scrubbing outside, swilling the yards – the toilet seats were white with scrubbing. And when everybody got new curtains the whole village would look bright and clean. Now they buy new curtains at any time.

□ From the hills a haze lies over the village. A grey blot on a rolling Yorkshire landscape. You know you are getting closer as the roadside grass changes from green to black – a metamorphosis – the result of a constant barrage of coal dust falling from the constant stream of lorries emerging from the colliery gates.

Black fronted houses set back from black coated kerb stones. The few shops look drab. The advertising hoarding vainly attempts to persuade the residents to buy *The Daily Telegraph*. It's like a dog barking up the wrong tree – except there aren't any trees.

It's been five years since the miners' strike. The estate lies like an open wound, sore, not healing, not recovered. Long grey terraces. Some houses empty, rubbish piling up in front gardens. Broken glass scattered, left where it exploded on the road. The wind whistles round the corners as it always does in these places.

Houses for sale but no buyers. 'Much sought after' and 'Highly desirable', these stick in the throat of even the most determined estate agent.

An infestation of rats in the dyke causes concern. The appearance of these rodents in peoples' houses creates alarm. The Health Centre is fighting a battle against an epidemic of head lice in local children. Another generation forced to scratch.

□ The ethics of a caring community seem to have been long forgotten and looking after those that are less able to look after themselves is now seen as unfashionable. A popular view seems to be that bad families have bred bad kids but this only serves to push the poor further into the poverty trap, which must be wrong. Responsible middle class society has deserted places like Grimethorpe.

□ There was an area of Cudworth called Sidcop, a bit rough but full of lovely people, some of them were real characters; Polly Bowen, she was a bookie's runner, Percy Rowbottom, he'd a row every Saturday night. There the midwife smoked a pipe and wore a flat cap. The off-licence was owned by the two Miss Wrights, real ladies they were; they went to church every Sunday night. There were no proper streets down there, they were just earth, and there would be hens clucking in and out of the houses. The people were smashing though, the best givers in the district and they did a lot for the local hospitals.

□ I lived in Beech Avenue for 45 years and from my bedroom I could see Sidcop. I used to like watching the hens going into the houses. Saturday night was always a thrill with the men shouting and fighting.

□ I suppose you have to admit that Grimethorpe has had its share of rough and tumble and it still does. I remember them telling the tale about the sinkers' boss who went into the top boozer and offered a gallon of beer if anybody could fetch him to twelve quiet men in Grimethorpe. A bloke took him up to the graveyard up White City and said "There thy is, that's t'only place tha'll find 'em round here."

□ On Saturday nights when they'd been fighting they used to cart them up to Cudworth Police Station in Danny Oates' ice cream van. In return, or so they say, Danny used to get the contract for providing ice cream at the police ball.

The last time she wore the conductor's cap

□ They had a head lice epidemic in Grimethorpe last year, they say it was

Steve McClarence

Grimethorpe Neighbourhood Centre

caused by the hot summer. A lot of people blame it on being mucky but it's not true. They don't go on dirty hair, it's too greasy for them and they can't keep hold so they slide off. They can jump though and that makes you mistrust your neighbours. Both families on each side of me got nits and it made me frightened to go and talk to them. It's a funny situation to be in especially when we're normally in and out of each other's houses having a kall. There aren't any nit nurses in the schools now either, they say they can't afford them, so you've to be constantly on your guard. I spent every morning and night last summer checking my youngsters' hair. They give free lotion out at the clinic but people still get embarrassed about things like that.

□ I used to have to get down on my knees every night after school with my head on mother's lap, "Come on," she'd say, "let's have a look in your hair." Them that had nits always had to sit in one part of the class with their head shaved. That's why I always had plaits.

□ If there's one thing that gets rumours flying about in a close knit community it's head lice. It starts off with getting pulled out by the nit nurse at school and if you're not careful you'll get the whole neighbourhood against you. It happened to our family, first they accused us of being mucky, then they said we were forever scratting and then they started saying our mother never gave us anything to eat and sent us to school in the clothes that we slept in. None of it was true but they ended up sending the Cruelty Officer, the Health Inspector and the Medical Officer round to our house. They checked the beds and examined us and found a big bruise on my shoulder. They wanted to know if our father hit us. I thought everybody's father hit them but when it turned out, I had rheumatic arthritis.

□ Our Pauline's little mate came in and

A close knit community

Steve McClarence

Rats in an English Surburban Garden

was playing with something in his fingers, I thought it was a bogey out of his nose but he said, "It's a 'dicky-bird' out of my hair, Aunty Hilda." That was the last time I let Pauline wear his conductor's cap.

□ Our Ernie, my cousin, once copped us smoking Craven A's after he saw smoke coming out of cracks in the aviary wall. My dad kept canaries and we used to go in his aviary out of the way. Ernie said, "Either I leather you now or your father does when he comes home." He was like that was our Ernie. So I said, "You best leather me now then." He was a bit strict was our dad you see.

We once went round knocking on people's doors asking for a 'Penny for the blind'. We'd seen somebody else doing it, so we got this tin and went all over Grimethorpe. When we got back we were counting the money out on a window sill when Dad caught us. He dragged us round and made us hand every penny back. It was only mischief we got up to then, though, knocking on folks' doors, breaking windows and tipping dustbins over, that sort of thing.

□ When you see the rubbish thrown about down the backs it doesn't half dishearten you. It only wants one or two and it spoils it for everybody who is trying to make the place look a bit nicer. We are as responsible as everybody else for our environment but it's a lot harder when you live in Grimethorpe.

I'm sick of having rats in the garden, the ratman's fed up of coming as well. When I got my new suite I put my old one out in the garden until they came to pick it up. When I helped them to lift it, out jumped a rat. It was the same when we first moved here; I put the shovel in the bunker for some coal and fetched it out with a rat on. Now I always lift the lid up and have a look first. I'll say this though....the next rat I do get it's going through the Council letterbox.

Drawing a veil across the urban environment

☐ I'm trying to encourage people to socialise again. They're welcome to come to the neighbourhood centre here in Grimey to sit down, make a pot of tea and have a kall. One aim is to make it a change from sitting and staring at four walls at home, and another is to put some spirit back into the community. Since the strike and with the rise of unemployment, a lot of the spirit has been knocked out.

Corner shops aren't social centres now that tinned stuff and ready cooked meals have caused people to believe that they haven't got the time, so they need replacing with an alternative. I wouldn't like it to get to a stage where neighbours start to get wary and distrust one another, hiding themselves behind curtains from the rest of the community. It saddens me a right lot when I go past some houses on a morning and see the curtains shut, because you know it means that they're either still in bed or the sun is shining through the window onto the television.

☐ My house has become a prison and it's as though them on Radio Four are my jailors. I get round to the Legion for a couple of pints now and again and ask anybody that's going past to give me a hand up the steps, but it's no fun when you've been used to leading an active life. I claim to be the youngest collier this century. At sixteen I was six foot and twelve and a half stone. On the coal face they called me 'the boy collier'. It was better than being a market man, I was paid straight off the note like other older men. Not bad for a lad who had pulmonary – that's first stages of consumption – as a toddler. I was that bad then that this Australian, called Dr Curtain, told my mother and father they'd to keep me away from school.

☐ We used to play a lot in the Square. In one house there lived a bloke called

Steve McClarence

"It doesn't half dishearten you"

Longman, his wife and daughter. We'd been having a game under the lamp when one of the lads came and told us he had seen old Longman doing some sewing on the sewing machine, so we jumped over the wall and looked through the crack in the curtains, and there he was sewing away. In front of the window was his wireless set; one of the lads said he made the wireless set himself. In those days they used to sell Oxo cubes in small tins, well, that wireless set was full of Oxo tins. You had to have an aerial wire and earth wire. The earth wire ran from the wireless and was buried deep in the front garden. We stood watching him sewing away and the wireless playing Henry Hall but when one of the lads knocked on the front door, we all flew! One of the lads got his foot fast in the earth wire and ripped it out. You've never seen as many Oxo tins flying about!

□ Now that everything comes in packets and bags there's bound to be more litter – nobody is burning it either. Course dogs will pull the bins over when they smell them.

□ We could all start by cleaning up the streets, they're a disgrace compared to what they used to be. When Johnny Barrons was on street cleaning, the pavements were clean enough to eat your dinner off. He took pride in his job and his dignity was such that he never felt belittled in doing what some would call a menial task. When dressed up he was one of the smartest men round here, always a bow tie and a nice cap and his prowess in mental arithmetic was unmatched. He could reckon up faster than a ready reckoner. He also had the loudest voice of any man I've ever heard, you could hear him coming three streets away, even when he whispered he could bust your ear drums. Our fathers and grandfathers would turn in their graves if they could see the state of the streets these days.

□ It makes me laugh when I see

Grimethorpe Schoolgirls c.1940

roadsweepers still going about with a brush and shovel, that's going back to Dick's days, they want to get some technology on the job.

□ With everything being throw-away it means there is less need for craftsmen but at one time in Cudworth there were some beauties. Mr Walter Guest was the funeral director, a Christian and a craftsman. You'd be pleased to go in one of his coffins. He provided all the handrails and chairs for the Methodist Chapel.

□ In the 1930s there was Father O'Shaugnessy, a ruthless Catholic priest who always walked about with a stick. He's been known to go in people's houses on a Friday and if they weren't having fish he's been known to swipe the meal straight off the table with his stick.

□ One thing I certainly do not miss from the so-called good old days is the discipline. I used to get caned for being late at school and I'd a three and a half mile walk every morning.

Sooner have a Shetland Pony

□ It's right what they say, when the characters go out of a place you start to lose the spirit and then the neighbourliness. Eventually it ends up where no bugger trusts another and people can't even be bothered to pass the time of day. There used to be a bell man from Blomfontein Street called Mr Holden, a very proud man when he told you what was going on. Then there was Teddy Thornton, the demon barber of Cudworth. Now there was a character. He once left me in the middle of a short back and sides to go and feed his pigeons. Another time he gave me a toffee and said, "Here suck on that while I have half an hour on my violin". He'd drink his tea while he was

Whitecross Road, Cudworth

working and sometimes there'd be half inch of hair floating on top of it. He hated cutting long hair, though, he used to say to lads with a mop of hair, "I'd sooner have a Shetland Pony sat in t'chair than thee." He once charged a lad with long hair 9d to cut it and another 9d next time he saw him in the street. One tale they always tell about him, is when Jacky Swann, a local boxer, dropped to sleep in his chair. Teddy went out it seems, and when he came back in the doorbell went and Jacky jumped up and started sparring.

□ They talk about characters, people are a product of their own environment surely, and who creates that environment? Or to be more precise – what creates that environment? I'll tell you what it is – Poverty! that's what. Poverty, exploitation and the need of other classes to keep us down.

Joe Burke's son was a joiner, he had a beautiful tool box that collapsed in two with the best tools in it. But every time he was thrown out of work he had to pawn them tools, although he made a proviso that he could visit them to oil them. Then he would take care every week to visit his tools and lovingly rub them down with grease. What a poor carry on that is.

Another was forced to be a bookie's runner through poverty. She'd stone flag floors in her house and no rugs and it was always full of men playing cards. Her daughter was a very wild looking woman with long grey hair, some people were terrified of her, but she'd had meningitis and she only wanted to touch you. She wouldn't hurt you. She got killed crossing the road to go to the bookies. What does that say to you?

Oh! how I miss my relief
More than I miss my dole.
I've a wife and six kiddies to keep
And only a bucket of coal.
The rent is coming next week,
To turn us all out in the street,
So stop aggravating
The workhouse is waiting.
Oh! how I miss my relief.

Steve McClarence

□ A lot of folk went to Lundwood after the big strike, the 1921 or 1926, and the pit stopped a shilling off their wages for years after. Them that had been on Parish Relief were paying back right up to the war. I walked to Hemsworth and told them I wanted assistance. Somehow they'd heard that my husband had done a bit of overtime the week before, so they wanted to know what I'd done with the money. Well, I'd heard about these men going in and banging their fists so I thought 'Go on lass give it a try'. They ended up fetching the bobbies to me and they told me to get on my way. I had to walk all the way back again without a penny.

□ They used to give us soup at school. I took a jar every day and filled it so my mother wouldn't go hungry.

□ They'd be examining your shoes and feet to see if you needed some new shoes. Some kids even wore odd shoes. My parents would never make me go out in odd shoes, they wouldn't stoop that low, so I went about in my bare feet!

□ There were two pawn shops in Cudworth, Top and Bottom. Nellie Kay was a fixture behind the counter in the top one. She was highly respected, a kind and delightful person who was a chorister and soloist as well as a Sunday school teacher. She never married, perhaps she didn't like men. When we went anywhere as girls we always took her as chaperone. "Going with Miss Kay" was a popular saying. We used to go to Roundhay Park at Leeds.

□ Norman Fellowes was a one-armed bookie's runner who had a good relationship with the police. Whenever they were going to pay a visit they would let him know and it gave him time to get rid of his slips. He used to go playing snooker in the West End Club and rest his cue on the brush bristles.

□ Frankie Gill knocked about

Shopping on relief

Market Place, Barnsley

around the top end of Cudworth always dressed immaculately and had a beautiful watch on a chain. If anybody asked him the time, it was always half past two. At least he was right twice a day!

□ Cipkins were Polish Jews and had a little wooden hut, where they sold monkey nuts and chewing gum. They used to let the front of the shed down and you could stock up with pop on the way to the Rock Picture House.

□ I'll never forget the day the Picture House in Cudworth burned down, they were showing *Tin Tin and The Frozen River*. Pity it didn't thaw out quick enough to put the fire out!

□ Jerv Nick – his proper name was Gervase Nicholson – ran the bug hut in Grimey. If you misbehaved he'd rattle you with his torch and his arm could extend six rows. Mrs Stewart, a Jewish woman from King Street, played the piano and she'd always got a packet of humbugs on the lid. Jerv used to strut about in front of the picture shouting 'Order! Order!' He was a deputy at Ferrymoor and the winder could always tell when him and his mate were on the cage because they were both massive blokes. They say he once sent them back down to get on the cage separately.

□ This business of the government selling water off reminds me of the old western films – one river in the district and them that live furthest upstream dam it off to prevent them downstream getting any. You can see what I mean, them at the top of the heap are always going to get the best. So what happens when private enterprise realises it can make even more profit by cutting back on water purification? Shall we all be poisoned?

□ The River Don rises above the

Winscar Reservoir then emerges from the reservoir through Dunford Bridge, Bullhouse, Millhouse and Penistone, then eventually through Oxspring, Thurgoland to Sheffield and Doncaster. In very early years, according to *Your River*, it was clean, unpolluted and full of fish.

In later years the Bullhouse Pit was opened and effluent containing iron oxide has ever since spilled into the river. During the early 1900s until approximately the 1950s it was impossible for wildlife or plants to exist. Since the 1950s, however, the river has considerably improved and the Yorkshire Water Authority has stocked it with fish. But come flood or storm, effluence from the pit still leaks into the river which becomes orange in colour until it runs clear again. Why does nobody accept responsibility?

You can smell the sea air from Cudworth

□ The West End Working Men's Club was for men only and as far as I know it still is. What sort of carry on is that? There are women round here that are better working men than any man. Our Elsie was a strapping lass, bigger than a lot of the lads and a better fighter. She played football and went swimming with them in the canal but woe betide any of them that laid a finger on her. During the First War she trammed on the pit top at Monckton but it was well known that she trammed underground as well; must have been the last woman down a pit in this country. She died of the big flu epidemic in 1919.

□ There's been quite a tradition of women politicians in Grimethorpe. Elizabeth Townsend was one of the better known, there's a street named after her now. Also in the 1930s there was a move toward an Independent Labour Party. They used to sing:

Vote Vote Vote for Mr. Broughton
Who's that knocking at the door?
If it's Stanley and his wife,
We'll stab him with a knife
And he won't come singing anymore.

□ The middle row of Victoria Terraces at Cudworth was called Bucket Row as all the houses had a bucket hanging on a nail outside the door. Whenever the lads came out of the club they would rattle the buckets with their sticks or stones and run up the ginnel onto the main road.

□ There are some interesting walks round Cudworth and Grimethorpe. The land is riddled with rabbit warrens, old pit workings and wells; even though most of the area has suffered through modern redevelopment it's still possible to see them. There are old claypits at the back of the Dards in Cudworth, this is where they got the clay to make hand made bricks which were used to build houses such as Victoria Row. The pits were filled in with refuse and when the field has been ploughed it's still possible to pick up Codd bottles. They're the ones with the marble in the top. A lot collect them these days.

□ In the same field there's a mound of a day hole pit, which I'm told was shut down during the 1926 Strike. It was covered with railway sleepers but a group of men including my grandad and his brother discovered it and removed the sleepers. After giving it a day to ventilate before going in to the workings, they set about getting out coal again. They were doing alright until a gang from Charles Street found out about it and wanted their share, but they started mining it from the drift side and fetched it all in. That put paid to it and the farmer filled in the entrance with wire and rubble.

It was very boggy at the bottom of the field and one day a horse owned by old Mrs Dable, who ran a shop in Charles Street, got fast. They say they had to put it down after they pulled it out because it was so worn out after its ordeal.

"The smell of sea air"

Down Weetshaw Lane there were two quarries, one on each side of the road. One was called Oakland's quarry; it was very deep, full of water and they say a few got drowned in it. On the other side was Methley's quarry and this had a lot of small ponds in it. All the local kids went down there for tadpoles and newts. Nowadays they have both been filled in with rubble and refuse. There used to be six houses in a row down there called 'the ratholes'.

□ My grandad told me about a plague of rats seen on Weetshaw Lane coming up from Oakland's quarry tip. A man was returning home from the railway on his bike, saw them and turned round to go another way. My grandad's best tale though concerned Gypsy Lane. He said if you went down there to what they called Whin Corner when the wind was in the right direction, you could smell the salt air of the sea.

□ Nobody could ever have dreamed of saving up to go to Margate and Brighton and places like that so they brought the names to Grimethorpe by giving the streets picturesque names. It was the nearest a lot got to the seaside.

Bing Crosby found in Cudworth

□ In Low Cudworth was the old Abbey Farm which the monks of Monk Bretton had when the Priory was going. They say two old stone coffins were found down there in the 1940s. An inscription on one of them said something in Latin which looked like *Bing Crosby*; he was popular at the time. The other one was broken up by a farmer because he didn't want anybody nosying about on his land.

□ Storr's Mill has still got an old stone bridge crossing the river but it's not in use since the road had to be altered to accommodate the railways. It's getting

"My Grandad told me . . . "

Storr's Mill

undermined by the river now and it'll be a great pity if it is left to collapse, as ramblers still use it. I would like to see one of those environmental pressure groups set to and repair it before it's lost forever.

□ The monks used to take a road called Ginny Lane between Snydale and Lunn Roads when they wanted to go fishing at the ponds at Ferrymoor on Grimethorpe Common. It's a swampy area now, what's left of it, mostly it's buried under the Coalite stock grounds. It was also the old route to Hall Steads, a moated manor house long since gone.

□ A Canadian came to Penistone and when he saw the stone walls he said "I just love your stone fences." Stone walling is a dying craft but they still have a class at the local ploughing match for stone walling. I think they have to do about two yards.

□ Going to Sheephouse Height Wood for a picnic and to gather blackberries one day we saw someone scrambling under a gate. They were being chased by a huge bull. However, we decided the bull was harmless and ventured into the wood. After collecting 12 pounds of blackberries I was boasting to a neighbour, an old Penistonian, and told her they were from Sheephouse Wood. She was most indignant and said she'd never heard of the place. She only knew a wood called 'Sheppusight', that's Sheephouse Height.

□ Place names can give a bit of fun. If you live in a place you don't notice how strange your home town might appear to outsiders. I was out in the car with a friend when he started laughing. "Is it really called Penis-tone?" he asked.

□ The old style landscape of the Penistone area has had of necessity to change in modern times. Formerly the fields were small and surrounded by walls

and hedges but then the-powers-that-be decreed that farmers should produce more food, milk, grain and potatoes, so farmers bought bigger machinery and built new buildings to accommodate more cows. In order to get into fields with this machinery, gateways had to be widened and walls and hedges removed to make bigger fields. It was not practicable for large machines to work in tiny fields because this meant more land wastage as more turning space was needed for machines. Farmers had to spend much of their capital to adjust to the new order. After a few years, they were told they were overproducing, there were milk lakes and butter mountains. "Take your land out of cultivation now," ordered the same powers. Farmers' problems should always be viewed with all this in mind.

□ We were always on the look out for any wild flowers, buttercups, daisies, milkmaids and marigolds – we called marigolds waterblobs. I was always on the look out for trembling grass which looked very well in any kind of vase. Today I am still looking for trembling grass.

□ In the war a subsidy was given for ploughing to encourage food production which resulted in the destruction of plants like orchids. At that time children from the infant school were taken to a nearby stream to watch the house martins collecting mud for nest building under the eaves of nearby houses.

The coal bondage

□ The good coming home feeling always settled in me when I reached the spot in the street where the coal lorry was usually parked – especially on a fine day. The large black patches with rainbow reflections around the edges forecast family harmonies around a brightly burning fire.

Wet or snowy weather could thoroughly disrupt the hard carefully balanced life-style, producing a frustrated hustling atmosphere. Then you endeavoured to coax the sulky fire to provide sufficient heat for water for the dirty workers, and bake great batches of cakes and bread, not to mention water for the washing of mounds of flannelette sheets. Washing would be hurriedly removed from the front of the fire when the master came home so that he could warm himself feet first, unhampered by the large clothes-horses full of sheets, towels and nappies. No disposable nappies; in those days people could ill-afford an extra shilling on the gas or electric bill or more than the budgeted oil for the stove. A full coal-house of dry coal was the best insurance policy for the winter.

Sometimes the quality of coal also gave rise to anxiety. A good load of coal at the gate, with plenty of large sparkling glassy pieces, and you could safely skip away again knowing that when you returned it would be safely stacked behind a dry-stone wall. Buckets filled for the night and crowned with sticks were dried in the oven top ready for next morning. In my younger days the household would hum in tune with the well ordered life.

Shale-free coal meant plenty of room for the mounds of ashes in the bin. They contained little else – no attractive designer packages; a treacle tin was the closest we got to stylish advertising. Papers from the packages of butter or lard were carefully hoarded for greasing and lining baking tins.

Meat was bought at the van at the door straight on to a plate or dish; milk into your own jug. There were no extra overheads for the vendors. Dirty root crop vegetables got tipped into a bag together with local grown fruit and the occasional orange or banana.

Tea or coffee also came without extra packaging. Beer was from the beer-off or jug and bottle and went straight into your own jug. Lemonade was in glass or stone

bottles, deposit or return, you never saw them lying around.

We were never allowed to forget to polish shoes. The uppers had to stand many times mending. We were glad of the flat round empty polish tins, they made wonderful hopscotches when filled with soil and glided gracefully across the concrete to land hopefully in the right square. Well battered, those tins eventually found refuge in the bin, as did the Germolene tin. More often medical care was home-based too. A covering of soft soap for bites, stings and blisters, a rub of butter for the children's bumps made do. Bandages were made from old cotton or linen sheets boiled with the Monday wash, ironed, rolled and re-used. Cough mixture was usually home-brewed and people's chests were well-greased with good old goose grease.

Few flies or insects survived the carbolic or tar-based disinfectants. Sinks, grates and toilets were cleaned with boiling water from the copper on washdays and sweetened with a scoop of washing soda bought by the stone.

The household was mother's domain and everything was organised so that there was no household work on Sundays. Friday morning was the fireplace morning and the woman of the house would be up by six o'clock, loosening the week's soot with an 'imp' exploding in the flues. Then the raking and manoeuvring of the flue brush into every nook and cranny would begin. Eventually all the soot would be gathered in the bucket to be used as insect repellant in the garden. Some people even used it to clean their teeth. Then the polishing and the black-leading would commence. When the room was spick and span, outside windows and sills were scrubbed and scoured and the housewife would skilfully decorate the edges with the colour and design of the donkey-stone of her choosing. Woe betide the neighbour who accidently fired the chimney after the Friday outside work was done. An unwritten rule was that chimney firing

was done after washday and before Friday, usually after dark.

Mother ruled the household but father ruled the coal-place and the garden, every inch of which was put to good use. The path was made of clinker riddled from the ashes of the household fire, the kitchen boiler or the greenhouse. We were never allowed to play in the back garden. It was full of vegetables from top to bottom. My father dug, planted and harvested. The one luxury he allowed himself were the red and white carnations and dark red pom-pom dahlias from which he renewed his button-hole through the summer. His last job before he went to Mind-your-own-business was to slick his hair with a minute speck of Brylcreem spread rapidly over both hands and then over his brushed back short back and sides. Singing or whistling, he surveyed himself in the mirror hanging in the kitchen window, took the button-hole from the frame above, settled it in his button-hole to his own satisfaction, straightened his tie, and off to the men's world where they talked of a fair day's work for a fair day's pay and a better world tomorrow.

□ For many years up to 1926 when the building of the Darfield Road estate took place, the road, or what was then a lane between Cudworth and Darfield, was only wide enough to be used by farmers, walkers and cyclists. On completion of the building of the estate, four or five one-man, one-bus proprietors engaged in competition in carrying of passengers to the main part of Cudworth and Barnsley. Both the owner-drivers and the conductors used ruthless means to get the passengers to travel on their buses, which were usually about 20 seaters with an unlimited number standing. There were no time schedules or recognised bus stops as such, and the driver would stop at 'the house with the blue curtains' or 'the house with the green gate' on request. The

Chara' Trip

competition was dangerous in that the drivers would race each other from cluster to cluster of people they hoped might be potential passengers. They'd race each other to Barnsley and back with no holds barred, forcing each other off the narrow roads into the ditches.

Later came the advent of the Yorkshire Traction with its better control of times and stopping places and its uniformed staff of driver and conductor. Even they couldn't control the environmental conditions of fog and smog that the district had to suffer because of being surrounded by collieries. Grimethorpe, Ferrymoor, Brierley, Monk Bretton, Wharncliffe Woodmoor and Carlton churned out their industrial smoke and dust to mingle with the prevalent fog of the times. Most houses were heated by coal supplied as a concession to the miners of the area, so smoke poured out of the chimneys to mingle with the already thick atmosphere.

Further, what wasn't and still isn't generally known, is that Cudworth's boundaries are water, on one side the River Dearne at Storr's Mill, on the other the dykes at Cudworth Bridge and on Grimethorpe Common. This continues towards Shafton and under the road which separates Cudworth from Shafton, down to Farfield and so back to Cudworth Bridge and forward to the River Dearne. The moisture from this, blended with the filth in the air, created the terrible environmental situation of the times. People very rarely left their homes when fog and smog prevailed. Then they ventured forth with the protection of an improvised face mask, usually a scarf or handkerchief. When taken off, this showed how much filth they would have inhaled without it. Bus conductors very often had to walk in front of their buses with a lamp or torch to show the driver the way. The railway which ran through the valley between Darfield, Cudworth and Carlton was often manned by fogmen doing their duties of security for the trains and warnings for the train drivers.

Bus crews had to contact the garage when the conditions got too bad and get permission to find their way home to the garage. Then they usually got home with faces as black as any miner.

At one time the miners from Barnsley and Monk Bretton travelled to Grimethorpe and Ferrymoor collieries in very primitive fashion, by train via Cudworth and Storr's Mill with open carriages, regardless of the weather. Later in this period the general method was by coal lorries fitted with a frame and stretched cover. There were loose seats down each side with a small ladder used for the men to get into the lorry from the back, this was a luxury.

The environment and these primitive conditions didn't change overnight, and only people over 70 years of age can visualise the wonderful changes from the bad old days. They are still grateful to the people who brought it about and gave us the comparable Utopia of today.

Kellogg's
SUGAR
FROSTED
FLAKES
Out of this world!

WASTE NOT WANT NOT

Eating your greens

□ These organic foods are alright for those that can afford them and for people who like to be fashionable but not for me. I'm a single parent with two kids under school age. I get £35.42 a week; £20 goes on snap, I put £2.50 in each of the kids' bank accounts and the rest goes on bread and milk during the week. Of course I'd like to eat free range eggs and cabbages grown without chemicals but I can't afford them. Instead I've got to put up with packet pies, fishfingers and baked beans. These make the kids feel sick and are stuffed with E numbers and colourings. Orange juice makes them hyperactive.

There's no wonder we're always at the doctor's and that's a job in itself. When I go to see the baby doctor I have to take bottles and nappies with me and feed and change the baby while I'm waiting. Sometimes it takes two hours and more. On occasions I've stood over an hour waiting for him to get weighed. You could say that nine times out of ten when I go to the doctor's I have to arrange for somebody else to pick my other youngster up from the nursery. I can't get anything done for waiting.

□ The doctors and medical experts these days talk about the need to eat plenty of fibre for a balanced diet. We used to bake Epsom Salts into the bread – that kept you regular. During the war when flour was harder to come by, I've seen me bake cold potato into bread.

□ There's three rooms and one doctor up at that surgery, so there's no excuse why we can't have more doctors. It's a bit ironic that in an industrial village where there's mucky air and a poor diet there's less doctors than there would be in say a rural village down south where yuppies live. If there was money in Grimethorpe they'd be here like ticks on a cow's back.

□ They talk about how health conscious people are these days about their eating habits. Don't believe them. Most kids I see going to school have obviously come out without a breakfast or a warm drink in them but they've got a bag of crisps in one hand and a can of fizzy pop in the other.

□ Family life should revolve around meal times. Now kids come home, take something out of the fridge and put it into the microwave.

□ If Maggie Thatcher was serious about family life she would pass a law to make sitting round a kitchen table compulsory. Sitting in front of the telly with a tray on your knee would be a capital offence.

□ Over the years I have noticed a change in eating habits. A grandmother asked her grandson what he wanted for dinner. "Chips," was his prompt reply. Grandmother started peeling potatoes to be pulled up sharply by her grandson. "Grandma, didn't you hear me, I said chips not potatoes."

□ I became a vegetarian partly for political reasons – think how much grain it takes to feed animals when it could be used to feed people – but mainly for moral ones. I just couldn't kill a little lamb even if I was starving.

□ We were clean but perhaps not up to today's hygienic standards. No getting bathed everyday for us, we got a good 'do' in the sink. But some of the stuff on the market now is a con trick. I've lovely hair and I never used shampoo. Gossinger's

Magical Soap was great – and you got coupons to get a free basin with it. No anti-perspirants and deodorants for me, and I'll tell you what, they're finding out now that they do more harm than good.

□ Organic food to me means plenty of good fresh meat on the table. There's been some great butchers in Cudworth. Johnny Walker was known as 'the people's friend', you'd see him at ten o'clock on a Saturday night shouting "Who'll give me sixpence?" and if you were poverty stricken he'd give you the sixpence back with your meat. Then there was Amy Brooksbank, she was as good as any man at butchering, if not better, as well as being a 12 handicap at golf. And there was Alan Frankish, Claude Mitchell and Silverwoods.

□ I became a vegetarian while I was working on a farm in Scotland picking blackcurrants. For lunch we had to kill two chickens and I volunteered. When it came to cutting off their heads I just couldn't cope. I forced myself to pluck them but from that day to this I've never touched meat.

□ There was a winder at Ferrymoor who used to buy bloaters in brown paper at Barnsley Market. He used to throw them on to a fire in the paper and when the paper burned off he said they were ready. He just used to scrape and gobble them. The smell was lovely, you could smell them a mile off in the pit bottom.

Wholly food and Co-operatives

□ Bon Watson used to open his front window and throw whole cods at you for about a tanner. He'd think nothing to coming round shouting for his money either, "Come from behind them lace curtains! You owe me a bob but you can have a tanner today." His speciality was the half crown parcel – bit of sausage, bit

'Well supported''

Steve McClarence

of liver and kidney. You could make do for a week at a push on that.

□ The Co-operative was well supported in this village. A big steam lorry used to come, they'd attach a pulley to the engine and lift sacks up into the storerooms above. When the ice man came he'd dump ice on the pavement and crack it up there.

The Co-op cheques and divi were very important. My mother used to save all hers on a big hook and she could tell you to within a penny or two how much she had to come back. They paid the divi out every six months.

It was a lot more than a shop was the Co-op. Chuck Andrews ran lessons at an evening school for them and you could get your recommends for hospital through them. Only firms that gave donations to hospitals could recommend. They had a convalescent home at Mablethorpe as well.

Eli Cooper's mother had eight beds and 24 lodgers, the beds never got cold. She got some right divi when she went. She used to buy whole hams and sacks of flour. When she baked she did it in a tin bath.

The flour lad at Co-op was called Bucktrout, he used to let me go in and get handfuls of Indian Corn. Aunt Mary on the other hand ran a general shop. All she seemed to sell was Beecham's Pills. Women used to buy five at a time wrapped up in a bit of silver foil.

Aside from the Co-op, the most famous shop in Grimethorpe was the 'pop' shop. Benny Dickenson ran it during the 20s and 30s. I've seen women come out of the top boozer and take off the clothes they were wearing and pawn them for a glass of beer. We used to get drapery on six month tick from the Co-op and Florrie Bailey, God bless her, used to take it straight round to the pop shop.

One of the butchers stored his chopping block and trestle tables leaned up against

"Cabbages as big as the gasometer"

my mother's dry middens. Flies used to be all over them. He used to give my mother a joint every week for scrubbing them. Mind, they were white when she finished.

The kids made a song up about all the shopkeepers, they'd go about the street singing

Old foxy John Horton,
Old piggy fat Bon,
Baldheaded Jim Ashton.

and so on and so on.

☐ My mother was one of a family of ten children who walked it from Hemsworth to Grimethorpe with a handcart for their furniture. When they got to Grimethorpe they wanted to make bread so they went to the Co-op to get flour on tick. The manager at Grimethorpe Co-op didn't know my mother so he wouldn't let her have any. This meant she had to walk back to Hemsworth again to get flour. On the way back her brother's feet started bleeding because his shoes needed mending and they say he crawled back part of the way on all fours.

☐ In the springtime a chap used to come round on a bike selling cabbage plants. He'd call out as he went past. Then there was Donkey Dick, he sold three caulis for a bob. It's famous for cauliflowers round here and they say Brierley broccoli is the finest in the whole of Yorkshire. All the gardeners grow it.

We had a little fat bloke who used to come round selling pikelets out of a basket and others who used to sell fruit. One used to shout,

"Bananas as big as lamp posts
Cabbages as big as the gasometer!"

Another one who came from Shafton, only used to shout "Bananas, bananas, ripe." A woman down Margate Street

Market Fresh, Barnsley c.1890

came out one day and asked for some and he said, "I'm sorry I've not got any today."

□ There's a lot of claptrap talked about healthy eating. Go in any supermarket and you'll see most food is junk, 'oven ready', 'pre-packed', 'bite sized pieces' – that sort of muck. They're feeding the hens on old carcasses, injecting their meat with chicken soup. There's mad cow disease, swine visicular and there's even battery pigs now. For all we didn't have refrigeration and to-day's hygiene standards, at least we had good quality fresh meat and we made good use of the scraps as well. Penny ducks, brains and udder – that was the milk bag off a cow. It was a yellow colour. They made it by boiling it, tipping it into a bowl and pressing it down with weights. The sweetest part of a pig was the chap – you'd call it cheek – that was beautiful. When we were at school we could hear the pigs squealing when they killed them.

□ Old Lass Stringer made nettle pop as well. As soon as she'd made above threepence she'd be off for a glass of something a bit stronger.

□ Before school we liked to call at Old Lass Stringer's house shop. She made toffee and flavoured it; so much with nuts, some with mint and some more with currants. Another woman used to make pikelets in a big copper.

The bus to Barnsley Market

□ Proper shopping had to be done at Barnsley Market on Saturday afternoons. There'd be buses all over, all shapes and sizes, and queues a mile long down from the top boozer. There was Taylors from Cudworth, Mills, Wrays from Lundwood, as well as Books, Maddisons, McAdews and Roses. One bloke had a Crossley. By hell that could shift. He could do two trips while the rest were doing one. They didn't

have any timetables and they'd stop anywhere.

□ People used to ask for landmarks when they wanted to get off the bus. You never hear anybody saying "A threepenny to the Blue Pig" nowadays. That was next to Butcher Holmes on Pontefract Road. Then there was another just up the street at the Post Office called Brooksbank's stop.

□ Traffic has ruined the environment more than anything as far as I'm concerned; great big lorries charging up and down shaking the houses, cars and motor bikes screeching about. It's becoming a nightmare to cross the road. Pontefract Road is just an endless stream of traffic now. We used to play cricket in the middle of that road, sometimes you could get through a whole game uninterrupted.

□ There must be something in the water round here that helps us breed good sports people. Dorothy Hyman was born in Blomfontein Street and Ernest Blenkinsop, who played at left back for Hull and England, came from Cudworth. He'd play professionally on Saturday and would catch the train back up to Cudworth to play at the back of the club on Sunday afternoon – thirty six players on each side and most of them in clogs. Des Flanagan was an amateur international and Steve Daly who played for Manchester City and Wolves was one of the first million pound transfers.

Butchering at home

□ Most allotment holders killed one pig per year for their own use. The method used was to contact the local pig killer,

who came along with a scratch, a sharp knife and a length of rope. The pig was tied by its snout and front leg to the scratch and its throat slit from front to back, a bucket was placed under the throat to catch any blood for black pudding making. My job from the age of five years was to jump up and down on the pig's stomach to force out the last drops of blood. You might have heard the saying 'We used everything bar the squeak', well, in Cudworth they even used that, squeezed into the baby's rattle.

□ The first pig in sow we could afford to buy was one at the end of its days but one with a very long pedigree. As soon as it attempted to get down to sleep we knew that there was going to be trouble. It would sway backwards and forwards, the massive stomach balanced on small rickety feet. There was no way of knowing which way it would fall.

Of course, my husband was on nights the night she decided to part with her heavy burden. She groaned and shuffled, stood up and flopped down again.

In the early hours of the morning I went down the yard to see how she was doing, clanging two metal buckets to frighten away any rats or mice, and found she already had a couple of piglets but was extremely nasty. She had snapped and had bitten one large piglet right across the top of its leg, so I reached over the wall with a brush and rescued the others as they were born. That done I stitched the injured one with a needle and cotton – about 17 stitches I think it was. After the eighth one was born, I pushed a dish containing two crushed Anadins and some milk towards her, still keeping her at the other side of the wall and using the brush.

In the morning she was happy and quiet again and I put the young piglets back, relieved when she accepted them so readily. Miraculously they all survived. At Christmas we had our first home produced pork. The stitch marks enhanced the golden brown crackling!

□ An old man said he could eat enough Yorkshire Pudding to flag a pig 'oil floor.

□ I used to go and watch my Uncle Harry kill pigs when anybody wanted one killing. Nearly everybody had a garden opposite North View. They stretched from back of the Picture House right down to the Catholic Church. When he went killing a pig he caught it and tied its legs together and got a seven pound hammer and hit it on the base of the neck till he broke it. You could always tell when he was killing, all the other pigs used to squeal for an hour or two. He used to slit it open, get all the innards out, then hang it up for twenty hours till all the blood had run from the carcass. Then he would cut it up; hams, sides of bacon, chops, anything that the owner wanted. They never paid much but he could always take what he wanted, so he always had a ham or a side of bacon hung up in the pantry or one of the bedrooms. It was an unwritten law that he could have first pick.

He also had a garden opposite his house and I used to go ratting with him. He had a dog called Spot. With everybody having hens and pigs, it was overrun with rats, so every so often he would take the dog and start ratting. The dog got nine rats in one morning.

□ I killed my first rabbit when I was about seven, my dad showed me how to do it. I'll never forget him up to his eyeballs in blood and drinking a glass of Kia-ora orange juice. The rabbit scratched my arm when I whacked it on the neck....it's enough to put a young lad off for life.

□ Years ago free-range hens were the norm. They involved much time spent in carrying buckets of food, water and corn, and also cleaning eggs. Farmers' wives, being more enlightened these days, find they can earn more money by doing other jobs than trailing round the fields carrying heavy buckets. To pay outside labour would be too costly. Hence there has to be the battery system, that is unless people are prepared to pay much more for their eggs.

I would like to see a return to the scenes of my childhood but farmers deserve as good a standard of living as anyone else. Rather than be a farmer's wife I opted to return to teaching as a more interesting and profitable occupation. We gave up keeping hens when they didn't pay on free range rather than keep them in batteries. We just kept a few on free range for ourselves.

□ Mrs Biltcliffe used to wash all the feathers off the hens she'd plucked and stuff pillows with them, and she used to sweep the hearth with the wing off a goose.

□ They made candles out of a tallow fat that came from mutton. There was a candle factory called John Moody's and a bone mill that made fertiliser and glue.

□ When I was a very tiny girl all of us children used to walk to my grandma's with our dad. I was so small I usually rode on his shoulders. Each Sunday morning Granny had the joint in the oven and it smelt glorious! We three little ones were sat upon the outside step and given huge chunks of bread which had been dunked in the joint's dripping. I loved it so much and always remembered it so I did the same for my four children. They still talk about it! Dad used to call the gravy which ran out of the meat the 'goodness', and each child starting with the youngest was given a spoonful on their dinner before Mum and Dad got theirs.

□ I've lived in this cottage in the main street for ten years now and have always, until last year, had a window box at the front with spring flowers growing in it for

Bridge Farm

Steve McClarence

"I love the view"

Easter, and either pansies or geraniums through summer to the autumn. Unfortunately, the window box was tipped up onto the ground three times by vandals whilst the bulbs were growing. I put them back each time but in the end I had to give up and take them round to the back garden. It seems a shame as they used to brighten up the High Street. The same thing happened on several occasions with my Christmas holly wreath. That's been used as a football and found in the middle of the road further up the street. Why do they have to spoil pretty things?

□ I love the view from the back window very much. You can't see a long way, it's all enclosed, but there is a cobbled yard and some ancient outbuildings with ivy growing profusely over them, a paradise for many birds. This is backed up by the most beautiful beech tree, a joy at any season. Many birds, including a pair of pretty doves nest there and visit my garden for titbits.

In their seasons a lovely white lilac and a graceful laburnum bring me much pleasure. Even washing up is a gift when you have the view from that window.

□ One third of the western economy is tied up in the motor industry but 60% of the pollution comes from car emission. If car manufacture was rationed severe unemployment problems would arise. More money should be put into the development of electric cars. We haven't come very far in 50 years from the electric milk float.

□ At Millhouse a windmill has been erected to provide power for local industry. It has been objected to by some of the local residents because of the stroboscope effect when the sun and wind are in a certain direction. The windmill is no worse an eyesore than the large electricity pylons which disfigure the landscape, especially those in the Snowden Hill area of Oxspring.

Tracking on the Dell

☐ People that come into the country complain about the cock crowing in the morning. Do they want to stop the dawn chorus as well?

☐ Farmers nowadays could not afford to pay labour to dig up weeds by hand, so what alternative is there but to spray?

☐ Organic farming is alive and kicking in Shafton. Just beyond the crossroads is our smallholding which for the last few years has been growing cereals and vegetables organically. Before changing over, like most farmers, we used all the modern technology like pesticides, insecticides and hormones to increase our yield. Always having doubts about this constant use of chemicals and their effect on the soil, the last straw came when asking for a chemical that we had used for years. We were told it was now a banned product because it was a potential cancer causer. That clinched it. We began to wonder what we were doing to the land and the food that we produced so our family decided to go organic.

Apart from odd times when harvesting, our family work the land ourselves. My husband is sometimes out on the tractor well into the night. The work is hard, the hours are long but the rewards are many, not least being able to eat good tasting, wholesome food containing no chemicals apart from what arrives from the heavens. We can't control the rain or the air.

The only livestock we have, about three hundred hens, are kept in rotation around the land, where in addition to keeping down pests and supplying eggs, their droppings are used in compost as the only fertilizer. They are fed on home grown weeds together with a supplement meal which, although not one hundred per cent organic, is classed as permissible by the Soil Association, the organic growers' society.

Much of our produce is sold to organic wholesalers although more and more is being sold in our own shop at the farm.

We have a regular clientele from the surrounding area. Out of season, they have to buy in organic food from other sources.

The whole family now eats organic food. We all like it and feel that we are healthier for it.

□ It takes three years to change over to organic growing during which time there is no harvest and therefore no income. If the government would help farmers during the changeover, maybe more farmers would consider becoming organic.

They don't tell you half of what is sprayed onto food. If they did, no one would eat it.

Most people blame the farmers for our horrible food today but it is supply and demand. People want clean, plump, plastic wrapped, supermarket food and that's what the farmer supplies. Organic food grown at home is relatively cheap. Small health food shops seem to keep prices down but the supermarkets are making a killing. If this food is imported, it's another excuse to up the price.

Lots of people buy from the farm in bulk, maybe for the week. People on special diets use our products. All our customers swear by the taste and quality of our food. Mind, it is not possible to get a purely organic egg. Hens can be fed on a meal containing forty per cent non organic feed and still produce an organic egg. Our hens eat organic weeds on organic land and pests fed on organic plants. It's the best we can do.

The Soil Association will allow certain additives to be used but they are very expensive so we don't use them here. Non organic farmers use sprays every year so never give the soil a rest. They spray for everything, even using preventative spraying. The land, carefully tended by generations of thinking farmers, is therefore being raped by today's profit seeking capitalists. Dustbowls are already forming in areas of Kent. How long can it last?

They tell us that wholemeal bread is good for us but the pesticides sprayed onto the cereal mainly rest in the husks. These husks are taken out to make white bread but left in the wholemeal. 'There's nowt taken out.' Who's kidding who?

Some people don't like our carrots because they're dirty and they will have to dirty their hands to prepare them. Those beautiful clean ones in the supermarket, wrapped in cellophane are so much better. Sprayed to make them grow, sprayed to keep off pests, sprayed to stop their growth and sprayed to keep them looking nice. I know which I prefer!

We once counted the number of sprays an apple gets before it sits shining on the shop shelf. We reckoned at least fifteen times. Organic apples may have a few blemishes but at least they are natural.

Our land attracts lots of wildlife including pheasants, partridges and butterflies. Our good food also attracts many rabbits, they know where to come; I've counted as many as eighteen eating our shoots. One year they ate six hundred in one night.

Broccoli, which is from the same family as oil seed rape, flowers just after the rape, so other farmers' black beetles leave the sprayed rape flowers to attack our broccoli. That's all in the game. Many crops are sprayed with chemicals so poisonous that they cannot be harvested for six weeks after treatment. Some that have been taken too soon have had to be thrown away. What a waste!

□ Did you know that insecticides were developed from nerve gases used in World War Two?

Organic farming is so small at the moment that the farming establishment laugh at us. We are a bit of a joke. Our time will come. Already the increased demand is causing some big companies to see the potential, no doubt with money in mind, but it's a start.

□ God only knows what we are putting into our children's bodies. Only years will reveal it and then it will be too late for some. We are seeing today the results of past radiation, asbestos and nuclear testing. They told us it was safe then and still won't accept responsibility today. Have no doubt it will happen again.

We don't keep our own bees but we seem to get lots of them in the summer. They too seem to know where the good nectar is.

□ I've eaten out of fields and woods when I've been hungry; blackberries, 'bread and cheese' that was hawthorn and red ripe berries. I've made coffee with dandelion roots and chewed cat nuts all day; they're white roots that look like nuts.

□ We used to be up at seven with our jugs in hand waiting for the milk to come from the Old Hall. It was still warm when we had the first drink. The first milk from a calf was grand, they called it 'beastlings' and it was like thick cream and very good for puddings and custard. Buttermilk, the residue from butter making, was marvellous in mashed potatoes and folk used to feed it to their pigs.

□ With new awareness of the environment, farmers are blamed for much of the pollution. However, they too are often sufferers. Whilst my brother was working in one of his fields, a stranger drove into the field and began to deposit a heap of rubbish. He was most indignant at being made to remove his rubbish as he thought the countryside was a legitimate place to dump it.

Another problem for farmers is the removal of stone walls, particularly the 'toppers'. Often yards are stolen to decorate gardens or build stone fireplaces. For some it is not regarded as stealing as they believe everything in the country is there for the taking.

My father understood the art of stone-walling and proudly kept his walls in good repair. He also saw to it that the hedges round his fields were layered. Modern hedge cutters just lopping off the tops made him shudder.

□ My mother was a great nature lover and many times bemoaned the disappearance of trembling grass. Whilst mowing hay my brother was startled to hear father shouting "Stop!" He stooped down and swooped up a swathe of trembling grass – the only clump in the field. He walked out of the field up the lane carrying the grass behind him then sheepishly presented it to mother who couldn't have been more pleased if it had been a bunch of roses.

With a carrier bag from Asda!

□ People took recycling for granted in days gone by. Everything had its uses. The rag and bone man came round the streets frequently – sometimes he gave coppers for rags, but in most cases he gave a small toy, a balloon or even a pot basin. Other old clothes were cut up into strips to make peg rugs, and jam jars and bottles were taken back to the shop to collect a deposit. Combustibles were burned on the fire either in the house or in the garden and sometimes we even chucked tins onto the fire in the house. They said it cleared the chimney.

□ When shoes were done a lot of folk made the fire with them. You can make a lovely fire with worn out shoes, they burn like hell. A person I know has a husband in the Fire Brigade and she says that the highest fire risk in this area is chimney fires. A lot used to deliberately set fire to them to clear the soot..

□ Potato peelings and vegetable stalks helped to spin out the coal allowance; piled up on the slack coal they helped to keep the fire in all night. All my organic waste these days goes onto a neighbour's

Steve McClarence

Grimethorpe Neighbourhood Skip

compost heap and my occasional reward is a sample of his onions.

□ Soot was good for use on the allotments but they used to put all sorts down to fertilize then. I know a man who poured a bucket full of blood from the slaughterhouse on to the roots of his grapevine.

□ It's not so much that we throw things away these days, it's that a lot of the stuff that gets thrown away is unnecessary in the first place. You don't see so many people with shopping bags now, so that means everytime they go shopping they get one of the plastic carriers. I remember in Cudworth when everybody brought their groceries home in their pinny, and if they were wrapped up in a bit of brown paper and string you thought you were posh. Brown paper itself had its uses. If you put a hot iron across it over clothes that were stained, it fetched the stains out. Try doing that with a carrier bag from Asda!

□ In 1916 one of the arches of the viaduct which carried the railway line between Penistone and Huddersfield collapsed. Nobody was hurt because the driver and the fireman jumped out when they saw what was happening. The engine was burnt up piecemeal at the river bank and they used the chimney from it as a plant pot on Denby Dale station for some years after.

□ Penistone station was always known as the coldest place on earth – it was the place that God created last. They say he'd left his tools in Barnsley.

□ Holidays in the late thirties were usually where you had a relative and I always felt I'd got a bad bargain – mine lived in Barnsley, whereas we lived in Sheffield and I'd been born in

Laying Tram Lines

Scarborough. However, an uncle moved to work for the BBC at Huddersfield and thus began a love-hate relationship with Penistone station. A halfpenny ride on the tram into Sheffield, the long walk up the station drive to get the train and then the gradual change of scenery from murky industry to the majesty of the moors. To a seven year old the church seemed to tower above everything especially in the frost or snow. We clambered out and scurried across to the waiting room to the blazing open fire, tables with white cloths, a cheery smile for two lone children and we were served with dignity tea and a snack before we boarded the train for Huddersfield.

Years later I whizzed past entrained for Manchester and looking up as the train paused at Penistone, I was glad not to have to stand shivering on the 'coldest station on earth'. Now I mourn amidst ruins for the cosy, friendly, strong-walled, clean waiting room and understand a little what motivates graffiti scribblers.

□ My chimneys were in danger of tumbling off after the big gales we had, so I had the stacks taken down – no need for coal fires now, is there? I saved the chimney pots, though, and put them in the yard with some flowers in.

□ I've done old hoovers up for years. If I hear about anybody throwing one out I go round and collect it. I've fitted new motors, I've made one out of three, anything. Same with irons and washing machines. The wife has still got an old washing machine with a winding handle for the rollers. I don't know how old it is but it's probably the one we got when we were married with other bits added. If I can repair it I will. I don't like throwing anything out.

□ Wheeltappers were employed to check the soundness of train wheels by tapping them with a long-handled hammer. If the wheel was sound it rang clear and true, if it was cracked it gave a dull tone. If a wheel was cracked the train was taken out of commission for repair. There's a story that wheeltapper Newt Hadfield had three trains in dock before he found out the hammer head was cracked! There's a moral there, somewhere.

□ Clothes were handed down until they couldn't be handed down any more, then they would be cut into strips and made into a peg rug after the buttons and zips were removed. The base of the rug would be hessian or even old coal sacks which had been washed. This would be suspended on a wooden frame made up of old bits of wood. The peg itself would be a sharpened clothes peg. Very often the work would be done by children after school, half an hour on the rug before they could go out to play. Often it was a source of income. Peg rugs wouldn't be thrown out, just moved from the hearth to the kitchen and then to the back door.

□ There were three mills in Penistone that made peg rugs. Two Whiteley's and Ogley's. They sold them to Great Universal Stores, that was the forerunner of these mail order catalogues. Mind, the best rugs have got to be those made by people for their own homes.

□ There have always been second-hand shops but today I think people go to them for different reasons. In the past people couldn't afford new so had to buy second-hand. Today it's really quite fashionable to buy second-hand furniture and even second-hand clothes.

□ During the war when the Germans were bombing Sheffield, they would fly over the village to get to their destination. After the raids they would take the same path home. One plane had engine failure and came to land next to Grimethorpe Wood. The pilot got out without a scratch and gave himself up to the police.

Then it was like the jungle telegraph. Word spread like wildfire. Before they

Laying a Lawn

could get the Home Guard to guard the plane the village people had been up to inspect it, decided the bits they would like and what they could make with it. Two hours later the plane was stripped of windows, doors, seats, the lot. It was a skeleton.

People made lighters, key rings and ornaments, from the perspex windows. Our family had the luxury of recycled leather seats without legs. They had been bolted to the floor of the plane.

□ One of my son's neighbours threw out two bikes for the scrapman. Instead of letting them go for scrap the scrapman fetched them over to me. Apart from buckled wheels and a few bits and bobs here and there that were twisted there was nothing wrong with them. It was a crime to throw them out. I did them up and my daughter had one and I gave the other to my daughter-in-law. I looked in the catalogue and one of them was priced at £134 – it was a folding one that you could put in the car – and the other was worth £85. They shone like new when I'd finished with them.

A few years ago I found an old lawn mower and some bike wheels that were no good. I took them home, knocked them together with some old packing cases and made a flat topped barrow. It saves some work that barrow, clearing rubble away from the house, taking bags of coal down to the kids.

□ When I was young I always kept breaking cups and as it was in the war you could not replace them so I had to sup out of a jam jar until I was fifteen. My gran had eleven kids and I used to say to my mum, "All other grandkids sup out of cups and they're younger than me." She said, "They don't break them."

□ If you buy toothpaste it comes in a tube....a perfectly adequate container. For some reason they put the tube in a box. Then when you pass the box over the

On the Scrap Heap

counter for paying, the sales assistant puts the box in a bag! What a waste of packaging!

□ I've always been conscious about waste. I never liked seeing things thrown away because of a change of colour scheme, mind or whatever. I became even more conscious of this during the strike of 84-85. Two or three second-hand shops opened up around the town and were chock-a-block with junk furniture, tools of all sorts and everything you could imagine. It was like Aladdin's Cave.

□ Quality Street tins were valuable assets. That's where folk would keep the Christmas Cake after it was made in October and before icing in December. It was also used for cloths, buttons and zips. Everything was salvaged from old shirts and clothes before being passed on to my dad for rags in the workshop. Good cotton rags could stay in the kitchen for floor cloths.

□ Clearing out my grandad's chicken house was a ritual. When the height of the chicken house floor had been raised at least three feet by layers of compacted chicken muck you then got the enjoyable job of rediscovering the concrete floor! All the muck was spread on the tomato beds in the large greenhouse when you had finished.

□ The Body Shop's got it right. You don't get all that paper but what I ask is this, "Are their bottles returnable?"

□ After the war we were still using clothing coupons. Clothes were a luxury. Garments were cut down to fit. We never threw any materials away. If it was faded on the right side, it was unpicked and the wrong side used. My pride and joy was a raincoat made out of barrage balloon material.

□ I always feel guilty about throwing

Environmentally Friendly

things out that I know have life left in them. I keep my clothes until they almost fall off me and I feel much better if I can repair something rather than abandon it to the bin. Yet it's much easier to tidy up the house if you can simply put all the rubbish straight into the bin. It takes effort to separate things out for recycling. I do try but I must confess that the occasional newspaper, quite a few jars and bottles, and certainly most of my tin cans, end up being thrown away.

□ When sheets got worn in the middle they were cut down the centre and the outside edges were stitched together from one end to the other. When shirt collars got frayed my aunty used to unpick the shirt collar, turn it round then stitch it up again.

□ I bought a microwave oven and when it came I got the sticky tape from the sides of the box to find another box inside. I opened that to find two large pieces of polystyrene and then it was wrapped in a large polythene bag. Wasn't this rather a lot?

□ Tights and stockings are good cut up to make stuffing for cushions. Rubbish is different from what it was thirty years ago. It was all paper carrier bags with string handles and cloth flour bags which could be used for other things. There weren't as many glossy magazines. There were no non-stick pans or tins and there were no nappy liners. People used muslin or terry nappies. Furniture polish was in round tins, applied with a rag and rubbed off with a duster. The soap powder is much improved as well.

□ People are much more environmentally friendly now. They aren't as ignorant and they're much more health conscious when eating. Litter is a very big problem but a lot of it could be controlled if the council spent a bit of money on putting up more litter bins. Many a time I've taken stuff home to put in my dustbin because there hasn't been a litter bin for miles. Also I've picked bottles up from the top deck of buses then disposed of them in a litter bin when I've got off the bus. Deposits on cans and bottles may discourage this kind of thing.

□ They used to tell us that nuclear fuels were a good thing but they didn't fool me. The real reason was that governments needed places like Windscale to make enriched plutonium for bombs. Now that we are entering a period of peace you'll hear less about nuclear fuels.

□ Green is now the colour but unless the Prime Minister gets down and analyses what it is really about – and it's not only about litter – then there's going to be real trouble.

□ Local government has to get their act together. They expect us to take the litter to the bank but who in their right mind will lug a carrier bag full of bottles to the bottle bank if it's miles away. To be environmentally conscious you have to be middle class with plenty of room. You also need a car. I suppose if you throw an iron bedstead in the garden it will rot down but it takes time.

□ Recycling is only another drug to alleviate a symptom. It won't provide any answers to the basic problem but given that we are too greedy, too selfish, and we consume too much, then being realistic, any initiatives that reduce the impact of all of that are to be encouraged. We can all involve ourselves in some small way – take our bottles to the bottle bank, paper to the paper bank, cans to the aluminium recycling centre. If there isn't one, tell your council and local supermarket that you want one. Don't pick up another plastic carrier when you leave the supermarket, instead save and use your old ones. Don't

Cat Hall Quarry

buy products that come in over-packaged wrapping and insist on returnable glass containers instead of environmentally damaging plastic ones.

There is so much that we can all do, if we can be bothered to turn away from the TV and think about it, get off our arses and do it. Who knows? In time a new consciousness may grow in which we recognise that we don't need all this stuff and that there's a world out there that has been pretty good to us, and that maybe we should take better care of it.

It may be that only when we humans have reached the point of imminent disaster will we realise that we have confused standard of living with quality of life, and that all we had was a standard of superficial affluence which denied the existence of another kind of richness.

□ I knew a chap who brewed his own beer. He always boiled the hops in his wife's support stocking. I always wondered if he washed them first.

□ I never throw zips, especially long ones, and buttons away. I keep them in an old tea tin. Same with screws, nails and pins; I keep them in an old enamelled bread bin.

I even recycled my aunty's old button tin. It was a tin that had once had an old mop head in. It's got written on it 'O cedar mop'. She kept buttons in it for years and when it got battered she started keeping nuts and bolts and screws in it. Then one day she was going to throw it out so I swapped it with her for a modern Rowntree's chocolate tin and we've still got the old Cedar Mop one. My girlfriend keeps bobbins of cotton in it now.

□ In the future will people be digging for plastic containers, tin cans and polystyrene or will they have found a way of making things from compressed paper or papier mache? What will the people be wearing? Plastic suits and smog masks to get them away from the smell of plastic backed disposable nappies? Will green

wellingtons still be around or will clogs be back?

□ These cleaning agents are supposed to kill all known germs – why? Some so-called germs are alright.

□ We lived in a terraced house so we never got the opportunity to enjoy a garden. My dad wouldn't be beat though. He collected soil and horse muck and emptied it into a border he'd made around the back yard. Then he built a cold frame out of old windows and grew flowers in it, night scented stock and marigolds. He kept a pair of toads in the frame so we never got problems with greenfly. At the side of the frame he kept an old peggy tub half full of horse muck and the other half water. He used that as liquid manure. When it lost its strength he'd top it up with fresh horse muck. He knew he needed fresh when he walked past and couldn't smell it.

□ I have one of those old stone bread bowls in the yard. It's older than me. All the glaze has gone crazy but it looks lovely full of soil and plants.

WHERE HAVE ALL THE FLOWERS GONE?

Wick with wildlife

□ It's better to look at green than black when you have to live in a place that's got a lot of industry. Private enterprise won't bother so much with grassing slag heaps because that costs money and them blokes don't want to be spending money for getting nothing back.

Whatever else you might hear these days, nationalisation was the best thing that ever happened to coal mining, particularly in the environmental aspects. Now we've got green mountains instead of black ones because they've grassed over the slag heaps. I think the first to be camouflaged like that round here were up near where the Coal Board workshops are now. Brierley muck used to be fetched down what they called the 'jinny' line. It was an endless rope that pulled eight tubs a time by a big friction engine. Nowadays the line is gone except for iron sleepers here and there. Folk walk their dogs up there now, it's a sort of unofficial public footpath.

□ There was a viaduct on that jinny line, we used to play football under it. Now and again, when the ball went up, we'd have to get up and fetch it but we'd stop the tub train first. We did this by using exactly the same method as they do down the pit – rapping on the line. We used to pull a saw blade or knife across two wires to make a contact and that signalled the driver to stop.

□ The countryside round Grimethorpe is really beautiful but it's being eroded more and more. The Derry fields were an absolute picture, now they're buried underneath the pit stacks. It was wick with wildlife down there; marshland flowers, frogs, kingfishers; an artist could have got his brush out down there. He couldn't now though. But I can still see it as plain as a painting.

□ As a little girl I lived in the last thatched cottage in Cudworth but they stripped the thatch off above sixty years since when the landlord wanted to replace it with tin. At the back of our house was a stream; we used to take our shoes and socks off and paddle in it, else collect frog spawn in jam jars for the window sill. Our mother hated them but we loved watching them turn from tadpoles and grow legs and turn to little frogs. There was an orchard nearby and we used to go nicking apples; two would keep watch while the others would climb the tree and shake them down. The farmer would come and run us but his old legs were nowhere near fast enough to catch us.

□ It makes you laugh. Whenever they want to show a typical idyllic English country village they always go down Dorset or Sussex or somewhere. Then it's always like a chocolate box, thatched roof cottage, whitewashed walls, roses climbing up outside and a cat sat on the mat outside the front door. They want to come round here and see the power station and broken glass and dog shit in front of the houses and rats in the dyke. That's typical England.

It's just not cricket

□ If there's one thing that sums up all that's nice in the English countryside in the summer time it's the game of cricket; the thwack of leather against willow, a pocket full of sandwiches and a can of ale. I've watched Grimethorpe this summer. It's only half an hour's walk from my front door in Cudworth to the gates of the cricket field. This season as I made my weekly pilgrimage I took time to look around and consider how much this walk across the common had changed since I made the same journey as a lad. Is it me that's got bigger or is the common shrinking? You don't have to look too far for the answer, those space invaders of industry have engulfed a lot of it. Where there used to be a hedgerow there is now a perimeter fence that makes you feel like you're walking past a prison rather than a pityard. Where once was a country lane is now a black mud laden road and instead of hearing birds and bees and children on bicycles all you hear is the thunder of enormous lorries. That part of the common is no longer a quiet stroll, it's become somewhere that you pass by as quick as possible, a place where you enter a tunnel wearing a white shirt and re-emerge wearing a polka dot one. Of course the masters of industry will tell you that they have to destroy such nice places in order that the community can survive. To me that's like amputating a leg when you've caused the injury in the first place.

If you sit by the pavilion at Grimethorpe on a sunny day there's no better place to be. Players and umpires in Persil white flannels and shirts, rolling hills and woodlands in the background, you could be anywhere. Then you look from the other side and see the rolling waste heaps and as fast as you can shout "Howzat!" you're back in Grimey. Personally I prefer to sit at the Pavilion end.

□ I captained England before I was ten and before I was eleven had played twenty matches at the Cudworth Oval. Our coal bucket came in for some fierce pace bowling from some of the fastest fiery Freds Darfield Road has ever seen. I can see it now, "Sobers to Boycott and oooh! a most elegant cover drive from the Yorkshireman, it's gone straight out of the garden, over the Darfield Road and is rolling at some speed in the direction of Grimethorpe power station."

Steve McClarence

□ Our favourite pastimes were going ratting in the dyke and bird nesting. I remember an incident one Saturday morning when one of the lads spotted a nest on some broken branches that were blocking up the dyke. We all tried to crawl along the branches and, of course, the inevitable happened. The branch groaned under the weight and down we went into the black shiny morass. We tried to clean ourselves off but only made matters worse and eventually we had to pluck up the courage to go home. When our father saw us he went stark raving mad, stripped us there and then in the back yard and got the bath down.

Jumping across the dyke was another of our pastimes. Come to think of it that usually ended up with us coming home to get a rollocking and an early bath as well.

The battle of Storr's Mill Wood

□ In Grimey they called it 'Dastering over t' dyke'. That was when you were dared to jump over certain parts of the water. 'Daster' was local slang for 'Dares t''. In proper English you'd say, "I dare you." Bird nesting was the best hobby. You don't get too many different kinds of eggs round here but the excitement of finding a nest with eggs in far outweighed the disappointment that it might just be another song thrush's. The ecstatic screams of, "It's a four egger!" from a scrawny youth stood precariously on a thin branch was like music to the ears.

There were many unwritten laws to bird nesting. One said that you should always leave so many eggs in a nest so as not to frighten the mother from hatching, and if there was only one egg in a nest you should never take it. All the terms of speech we used were special as well: A 'laggy' meant it was a nest from the previous year, a 'builder' was a nest that the mother was still making and a 'ragged 'un' was a nest that had been destroyed by lads who took pleasure in such things. When we found a broken egg we called it a 'posher'. We had special names for some of the birds as well; 'cuddy' was a hedge sparrow, 'spoggy' a house sparrow, 'sheps' were starlings, 'skallys' skylarks and 'chivvy' a linnet. You don't often see skylarks these days and I've read that the song thrush is one of our rarest garden birds these days.

I remember on my first trip alone to the bluebell woods I found a partridge nest with six eggs in. To a kid of eight who had previously only found mucky old starlings and hedge sparrows it was like finding and opening Pandora's box in our back ginnel. By the time the story got round the nest contained twenty four eggs and seventeen lads from our backs were planning an expedition to get one for their collection. Loaded up with old lemonade bottles full of water in case we got thirsty on the way we set off. On arrival at the woods we couldn't find the nest again. Then half of the expedition started to complain that the nest probably didn't exist in the first place and to make matters worse we got run by the gamekeeper half way home.

□ My first memories of breaking out into the countryside are of being shot to ribbons by enemy soldiers in Storr's Mill Wood on the outskirts of Cudworth. Of course in our war games we were immediately reincarnated as a different soldier; if only all wars could be fought by people under the age of ten. Once we decided who were the goodies and who were the baddies the chase would be on through the trees and nettles, foxgloves and rocks. This could be Burma, Africa or anywhere for all we cared. All Saturday afternoon mouth-made gunfire could be heard ringing out from the undergrowth. The following Saturday those woods would become Sherwood Forest and the arguments would start as to who would be Robin Hood, Little John and the Sheriff of Nottingham. Sometimes we'd even let a few girls join in to make the numbers up in

Steve McClarence

Volker Bredebusch

the band of merry men and of course we always picked a nice looking one to be Maid Marian. At weekends and during school holidays we virtually lived in those woods. It was mysterious and eerie and full of adventure; in those days they seemed to stretch for miles. An old disused single railway track runs through the wood and many is the time I've seen a platoon of soldiers or the sheriff's men ambushed there.

Come the evening the bedraggled soldiers would wearily make their way home after a long day's battle. What a bunch of merry men we must have looked, all T-shirts, snake belts, sneakers and snot, carrying DIY bows and arrows and spears. As we neared home the twilight chorus of mothers could be heard, all shouting home their hero or villain, "Mich-ael" "Da-vid" "Su-san". Then off would come your wellies and leggings and you'd be stood in the kitchen sink for all the world to see while your mother washed your legs. Then because of the nettle stings and insect bites they'd itch like mad but that would all be forgotten when the call to arms came again on the following day.

Woods aren't just for bird spotters and picnickers, they're for soldiers and knights, gallant heroes and fair maidens. We lived, died, laughed and cried in those woods.

□ One of our ancestors was Mark 'Merry Legs'. A lot called him that because he went wherever his legs carried him. He loved the countryside and tramped all over the place. They used to say that he'd go out of his front door and throw his cap up in the air and whichever road it landed, he'd head in that direction. He knew the signs of tramps and gypsies, where to get a meal and a head down for the night. They once fetched him back from Stoke-on-Trent because he'd worn his shoes out and his feet were that bad he couldn't walk another step. Some folk called him 'Mutiny' because he'd organised a mutiny during the First World War. He used to fetch bodies off the battlefield.

Farmers, vandals and trespassers

□ Our family have been farming in and around Cudworth for years. We lived at Hawthorne Farm in Shafton. I remember well the smaller fields which were well manured by organic methods and the amount of labourers we employed. Sometimes there were as many as twelve men to feed and no machinery. Nowadays the fields are much bigger and the hedgerows are disappearing fast. I would say that farmers around here have tried to adopt a sensible attitude towards the problem of pulling up hedgerows and turning meadow lands over to the plough but we're fighting a losing battle against hooligans. They pull fence posts up and allow cattle to stray. We've recently had to get shut of some cows and turn some pasture land over to crops because we were so fed up with vandals. And there are people who are not farmers coming into it now, scrap metal merchants who wouldn't have the first idea of how to grow grass.

□ These people who rip up hedgerows and destroy long established fields and meadows should consider what they're really doing. Every year in Britain it's happening more and more and Cudworth hasn't escaped this onslaught as I have witnessed myself. Fields that I knew as a lad with lady's smock, harebells and meadowsweet and hosts of other flora have been destroyed for a few extra pounds to the farmer and a loss forever to the future of Cudworth. One of the saddest losses of recent years was a field that had never been ploughed in living memory. Generations of men and women would go there collecting blue stalks; their darkened rings plain to see in the early autumn. Now that has gone. Near to it is a little patch of southern marsh orchids but I wonder for how much longer? Will they become as rare to us in Cudworth as a meadow cranesbill or marsh marigold? When did you last see a wild pansy, wood violet, forget-me-nots or clustered bellflower? These would have been common to our grandparents. What will be left for our grandchildren?

□ A lot of youths have no consideration for the countryside; they don't get the discipline and instruction on how to treat things properly. They leave gates open on land that they shouldn't even be trespassing on in the first place.

□ The council must have spent a fortune putting new signs up to let folk know where these old footpaths are. There's a farmer round here that keeps pulling them up everytime they put one in place. I know what his game is. He's trying to redirect the path so that it goes over some marshy land that he can't put under the plough but you wouldn't want to be walking down there. I've seen water up to the top of the wall in winter. He keeps putting barbed wire up as well but the council keep making him take it down.

□ I was out walking in the fields above Grimethorpe and this farmer come up to me and said, "I'm sorry to tell you, but you can't walk here, this is private land and you're trespassing." So I come back with, "Well I'm sorry to tell thee young man, but I've been walking round here for nearly seventy years and I'm not going to change my habits now." At that I turned on my heel, walked straight over the field and left him to his shooting.

□ I've swum in the Dearne, you wouldn't do that now for fear of being poisoned, and I've walked up on Houghton Common when it was all bracken. You can't do that now because it's all ploughed in but the saddest loss of all as far as I'm concerned is Sidlow's Farm and that little stream that used to run up side of it. It nearly makes you cry to go down there and see how them slag heaps have crept over the land. We used to go trout tickling down there, can you believe that, trout tickling in Grimethorpe! I once told a bloke about it and he didn't believe me so I took him down and showed him. Talk about stunned, he turned round and said, "Well....if tha told me there was a bloody crocodile in there now I'd believe thee."

A lot of the country paths that were forbidden to us in years gone by have been opened up now and that's a good thing. We are only reclaiming what was everybody's in the first place but in those times the landowners were very strict. There were great iron railings round and 'Trespassers will be Prosecuted' signs everywhere. The Diamond family, who owned Barnsley Brewery, employed loads of gamekeepers to keep people out.

□ You'd be surprised at the number of folk who go walking up in the woods. You couldn't always go there legally, either, when them landowners were in charge. Old Tom Makin's gamekeeper has run us off more than a time or two. They're beautiful woods; when the sun shines on the ferns it's a treat to see. A relative of mine came from the other side of Leeds and he couldn't believe this was only ten minutes walk outside of a coal mining village. And when the rhododendrons are out, that's a real sight for sore eyes. There must be something in the ground for so many of them to grow in woods. People have taken cuttings but they can't get them to grow at home. You should see the amount of people up here towards the back end of August when the mushrooms start coming. The Poles and Yugoslavians come up, they know which fungus to pick up and eat and which is poison. I like to come up for blue stalk mushrooms, not so much because I like eating them, in fact I give most of them away, but it's a good

Steve McClarence

adventure coming up into the woods and rooting about for mushrooms.

□ Every year they plough over the footpath leading to the woods and every year the path comes back again like magic. It's as if people round here are sensitive as to where the path is. Folk like to come out of the smog to get a bit of fresh air and these days with a lot of the smoke gone, you can see Barnsley Town Hall on a clear day. If you look a bit closer to home, though, you can see bags of old plaster, empty paint tins, used carpets and black bags. Why they bring rubbish into these woods when there's a Dumpit site up the road is anybody's guess, but I blame these cowboy firms who are renovating houses.

□ Our lad is in the Grimethorpe Band, he takes his mouthpiece with him wherever he goes. He loves to walk up in the woods and you can hear him blowing. They need to keep their mouths right, with pursed up lips. He even takes it on holiday with him.

□ Bobbies' Jobs that's what they called good jobs. They were only kidding but it's true that them who were in the cricket, soccer or first aid teams and the bandsmen all got the best jobs at the pit.

□ There was a bandstand in the little park opposite the church and Grimethorpe Colliery Brass Band used to play there in the summer. A chap called William Foster was the leader and sometimes he'd get that excited he'd whip his cap off with the baton. There was a paddling pool at back of there as well.

□ We've got a river in Grimey although you wouldn't think so to see it these days. The River Tom it's called but it's not much more than a dyke. Nowadays it's full of old bedsteads, bikes and muck. Years ago all the kids used to bathe there, splashing about having a great time. Now you can't get near for the smell.

□ It was a great event when they opened the pithead baths at Grimey. A lot of people lined up to watch on the first day but some of the men still came home in their muck, preferring to bath in front of the fire.

□ We used to make our own lanterns, we called them "touch wood burners." We did it at the beginning of summer and they were very good summers then. Along the dyke, in front of North View we used to get some clay, enough to make a three inch square, then sit on the pavement for two or three hours banging away until the clay was as solid as we could get it. After getting a knife and taking the middle out, leaving the sides and bottom about a quarter inch thick, you would make some air holes in the sides and ends then place it somewhere to dry, either in the coal-place or in the outside toilet. There were no flush toilets then, all were dry and they used to empty them in the night. While the touch wood burners were setting, we used to go on to the Common where some old trees were, they were just past the gasometer but that has gone now. We used to get enough touch wood to burn for a couple of days, then go back home and get your touch wood burner out from where you hid it, put a bit of paper in a red hot coke – if your mother would get one for you out of the fireplace – and take it outside and sit there till you were called in for bed.

Another thing we did was to pick trembling grass and penny moons, a daisy-like flower.

□ Grimethorpe has never had any swimming baths and it's not for lack of trying, we've been campaigning for years. At least when the Tom was clear we could have a splash about in that. In the end they gave us a sauna bath. You can't swim in one of them, though.

□ We didn't have a bath but we used to help a woman called Mrs Akeroyd who

Steve McClarence

worked at Grimethorpe pit offices. She used to make the dinner and we used to dust round. Then we'd get bathed in the pit manager's bath with a clothes-horse round us.

□ There are some lovely walks round here but there were a lot more at one time. Rhododendron woods, penny moon fields – a lot of it is under the pit stacks now.

We walked everywhere; across the Common to a wooden hut that sold pop, and to Cudworth feast by Peg's orchard to buy a ha'porth of crab apples.

Before the big pits were sunk folk used to get coal out of the hedge bottoms but at least they left the hedgerows intact. It makes you sick to see what the farmers are doing now, turning everything in and putting it under the plough. Same with meadows; it takes hundreds of years to make a meadow. Once you've destroyed one you can't just create another at the snap of a finger.

□ When we were courting the lads would want to be taking us up Pudding Hill and for so-called walks in the country. We used to tie 'tar band' round the bottom of our knicker legs. By, it was strong stuff you could have got into a vault easier.

They are making some effort to improve the quality of the environment round here but there's a long way to go. They packed the pond up at the Dell with fish and they're trying to encourage wildlife. Some mallards came, but there's already one without a partner. A heron came and somebody shot it. They found it dead in the reeds, a beautiful bird like that. Then there's egg stealing and it's not just young ones that do that, either.

□ The nearest I came to a farm or farm animals before I was married was on the Friday before Tatie Picking Week in 1944, the year before the end of the War. A group of people from the school got together to find work for the following week.

We went dressed to impress the farmer with our suitability. I would be ten years old and the oldest fourteen years old. The girls were wearing long brown or black woollen stockings (the only alternative at the time) held up with elastic and wellingtons over them. An assortment of old coats were topped with home knitted woolly hats and scarves and on our hands were old socks to keep out the cold. Only the oldest boys wore long trousers. It was a matter of economy – they only progressed into long trousers when they looked too stupid in the short ones.

Our enthusiasm was completely squashed. Only a handful of the older boys were chosen.

□ The chap who took the night soil in his horse and cart lived in a terraced house next to my friend. He grew the most beautiful gooseberries, the biggest I'd ever seen. One day we were playing down the garden and helping ourselves to the gooseberries, when my friend's mother came along and told us why the gooseberries were so gorgeous. Needless to say that was the last time we helped ourselves.

□ When I was in the Land Army we used manure from the slaughterhouse, not just the usual but rotten carcasses, bones, offal... the lot. The man who taught us muck spreading used to say, "It's all done with a flick of the wrist." Consequently, I finished up with half the muck on me, after which I was very poorly and sent home on sick leave. So much for organic food!

□ Gardeners and allotment owners round here have always improvised with fertilisers. It's passed down from father to son, they know what's good for the earth. I carry on the tradition and some say my compost heap is the most glorious in Cudworth. My father used to collect poultry droppings from all over and place them on a two foot square plate under

Grimethorpe & Cudworth Library Staff

which a fire was lighted. When the droppings became dry and crumbly he rubbed them to a fine powder and sprinkled it on selected vegetables like marrows and leeks. He won prizes with that powder. The compost heap for general use was composed of the usual animal waste, house waste like tea leaves and blood from the slaughterhouse; anything that would rot down on the heap. We were putting nitrates back into the soil before people knew there was such a thing.

□ I've eaten some stuff from the fields. Hedges, I've eaten bloody hedges, stacks of cat haigs, birds eat them. I've sat up in trees as long as I could eat them.

Six slices of brown bread with tatey mixed with oxo on. Cocoa with Lyle's Golden Syrup. Get that across your chest and you'll ail nowt.

□ I worked in the fields from the age of fourteen, chopping turnips till my hands froze to them and they nearly pulled me back into the ground. We used to go out on a big cart like a punt. It held over forty people and was pulled by two big shire horses. One day these horses shied at a donkey that Jack Marshall had fetched back from Doncaster market and over went the cart. The wheel went straight across my mate's neck and a woman's guts. Bad do that.

A lot came round in horse and carts. Briscoe's had one. He once backed it straight into the quarry when he was tipping rubbish. Linstead had a cart. He used to go to Barnsley market, load up with his stuff, get drunk and put the reins round his neck and the horse'd fetch him home.

□ Bailey's Circus used to come and set up in the church hall. They had no animals except one horse. Then there was a bloke with a tingalari and a dancing bear.

Where have all the earwigs gone?

☐ Oscar Wilde said fox hunting is "the unspeakable in pursuit of the uneatable." Well said that man, that's what I say. Those people who go chasing animals around the countryside for pleasure are liars when they say it is a necessary part of country life.

☐ In the autumn of 1962 we had problems with the foxes stealing poultry from the smallholding. On the last day of the year it snowed heavily and in the early morning of the New Year 1963, there was a sharp frost. At daylight we could see clearly the way one animal had explored all the outside huts and had returned unsuccessful in its hunting and left a clear trail of deep prints in the snow across the next field.

A bit later a fox, two vixens and several cubs were found in a broken drain close to the path from Three Nooks Lane to Shafton. One cub was kept as a pet, the rest were shot.

☐ There was an area called The Rakes, a pond giving in to trout streams, with frogs, newts and that. There were celandines, violets with long stems, spotted orchids and common orchids, blackberries and gorse. Canada geese came every year and ducks, hundreds of them. There'd be people up there pulling up watercress and fungus off trees. Partridge eggs, you could get sackfuls, and horse mushrooms, loads of them. You could have breakfast, dinner and tea. It could have been a beautiful wildlife sanctuary but they don't seem to care with it being Grimethorpe.

☐ At one time when you lifted a stone up to see what was underneath there'd be all sorts of wildlife. Insects like hardbacks and earwigs. Where have all the earwigs gone? That's what I want to know.

☐ It's all kill, kill, kill, with these insidious chemical sprays, fertilisers, insecticides and weedkillers. At one time you didn't spray flies you swatted them.

☐ I can't abide farmers for wanting to kill everything in sight, hedgerows, wildflowers, small creatures. At one time they used to be part of the community now they're rapidly becoming outsiders. They were contracted to shift the snow in years gone by and tip it into the dyke. They stopped doing it because they reckoned if they weren't wanted into summer, why should they be made to do it in winter?

Cutting trees down in Cudworth and Brazil

☐ We should all be aware of the decline in quality of the environment. It isn't just about chopping trees in Brazil and melting the ice caps. It applies to us in Cudworth just as much as anywhere else and it's ultimately our responsibility. Neighbours have pulled together in the past to combat social problems; there is no reason why the same shouldn't apply to environmental ones.

☐ The Greens are going to have to broaden their manifesto a lot. I've read it and I wasn't too impressed. Making people aware of environmental issues can only be a good thing but when it all boils down, their perspectives are too narrow. It's alright worrying about pulling trees up in Brazil but what they really ought to be worrying about is pulling this bloody monetary system up.

☐ A forest the size of Wales (that's 130 million trees), 6 billion bottles and jars, 11 billion food and drink cans, 2.5 million tonnes of plastic. That is what we, the British, throw away each year. A staggering 20 million tonnes that costs £1.5 billion in landfill and incineration disposal. Reclaiming and recycling this waste would put around £750 million back into the economy whilst greatly reducing the enormous amounts of energy required to produce the goods in the first place. Additionally there would be substantial savings in import costs of raw materials and products to replace the mountains that we have thrown away.

By any reasonable argument these figures illustrate a complete madness in current economic thinking. The opportunities for job creation in new reclamation and recycling initiatives are considerable. The reduction in the destruction of natural habitats and ecological systems would be significant.

What is it that has brought about this hugely damaging situation? Well, we have the rampant twentieth century consumer who has come to believe that 'wealth creation' is always progress. The consequences of our industrialism are the price we pay for our twentieth century lifestyle. Our dustbins are full on Thursday but by Friday someone has taken the evidence of our excessive consumption away and we can happily sit back to begin the process all over again. It is only now becoming clear that we might just have sat back too long and allowed clumsy ethics of the market place to gather so much momentum that it has become impossible to stop.

It is a wicked irony that the appalling environmental impact of our industrialist/consumerist society has been recognised through the efforts of that very technology that caused the problem in the first place. The new danger is to cling blindly to the old belief that the experts can employ yet further technology to solve the problems. We do still place trust in the political and economic systems to provide the fix while we sit back, secure in the belief that because it has always been that way then it always will be. Complacency is something that the British have traditionally been very good at. We only have to look around at the way in which we as a nation have allowed so much of

our heritage – buildings, countryside and communities – to disappear with hardly a murmur. If voices have been raised then it has generally been a cry from the ranks of the middle classes but rarely from those viewed as working class. Indeed it has been said that environmentalism is merely an expression of middle class guilt formed in the Sixties and Seventies during the wave of prosperity and leisure that allowed them the privilege of concern.

□ Peg's orchard was full of fruit trees, Siberian Crabs, Bell Pears, Marie-Louise and Conference. A paradise for kids round here.

□ Father rarely had a new suit, but he'd always a fresh flower. In the summer he wore a red and white carnation and come the autumn he sported a red 'pom-pom' dahlia. He looked immaculate going out to his Labour Party meeting with his red 'pom-pom' dahlia in his lapel.

□ I've voted Labour all my life but in them European elections I voted for the Green Party because my daughter kept pestering me. I don't think I'd vote for them in a proper election, though.

□ I voted Green at the European election (though I wouldn't in a national one) and phoned my MP to tell him why I did. "You watch," I said, 'they'll get a big vote and what that is is a democratic people telling you lot that the Labour Party is not much better when it comes to environmental issues than the Tories." I was right.

□ I got sick of hearing my daughter pestering me about using hair spray and underarm deodorant. I didn't know the first thing about the ozone layer and to be honest, I didn't really care. She kept on, though, and tormented my life out and I've gradually come round to her way of thinking. Yes, I could vote for the Greens,

Steve McClarence

"Can't see the water"

you've only to look at the funny weather we've been having to see that there's something up.

□ There's a lot of mileage being gained by political parties jumping on to the Green bandwagon but commercial enterprise is really giving it the hard sell. So-called health foods, low fat this, low salt that, and these tracksuit and training shoe people must be making a fortune. My daughter goes to these Dancercise classes, she keeps trying to get me to go but I should look alright at seventy-odd. I think there's nothing looks worse than old folk dragging each other round a dance floor and if I ever get as low as to sit playing bingo at a Welfare or OAP club, I might as well give up now.

Can't see the water for carpets

□ We certainly don't know enough about toxic wastes and poisons in the water and it's easy to ignore pollution because we can't always see it, until it has its effects. But when you see these fish upside down in rivers, then you can see what's going on. Perhaps it's a product of the more affluent society, the bugger-you-I'm-alright-Jack mentality. These big firms are pouring their rubbish into streams, grabbing the money and everybody else gets their crap.

□ Cudworth is completely surrounded by water, streams form the boundaries and dumpit sites, but just recently a woman was fined £200 for illegal dumping. What possesses people to throw black bags into the back of their cars, drive past their neighbours' houses into the countryside and throw muck into the hedge bottoms? It's anti-social behaviour and that's because nobody knows anybody anymore, especially from them who think that they've got on a bit and can afford new carpets every new moon. Social conscience is becoming an ever decreasing circle round here.

□ When you look at that dyke in Grimethorpe you can't see the water for carpets. They reckon that the water is clean when it runs in, but I can't see it being clean for long, not with the rats and smells that come off it. A youngster was drowned in it a few years ago. They wouldn't stand for it anywhere else. I suppose they think because it's Grimethorpe they can get away with it but they can't.

□ When they had that meeting at St Luke's last year Tricia Haigh, the Health Visitor, said she was concerned about children playing near the dyke as it was a danger to their health. It's rat infested, smells terrible and is unfenced.

□ In between Shafton and South Hiendley there's a maggot farm. I took my grandson out for a walk in Hawthorn Street and we were pestered with big blue-bottle flies from start to finish. It's terrible when you can't go out for a nice walk. I can say without fear of contradiction that if there are 9758 people in Cudworth 9757 of them will complain about the smell from the maggot farm.

□ I should say the three main things that pollute this village are the Coalite plant, the methane from the pit and the sewerage works. They make tar and chemical by-products at Coalite. At one time methane was drawn from the pits by a series of pipes and then a big pipe ran up over the head gear and fed out into the air about three yards above the pit wheels. Nowadays they burn a lot of the methane off but a lot of it still gets into the air. I don't know what you can do about smells from the sewerage apart from adding a drop of perfume.

Sewerages do have their good points though. We used to go down there picking tomatoes; you get lovely tomatoes down near sewerages. During the war a lot of farm machinery was run off methane gas produced at sewerages and off piles of pig muck and that.

□ Coal screening used to cause a lot of pollution, muck flying everywhere. It was more like dry cleaning than the washing that they do these days. The biggest irony of all though is the fact that they are making the village a smokeless zone while the Coalite plant is still pumping it out.

□ It seems a bit daft to say it but in a lot of cases I don't blame people for dropping litter. How can you criticise them when they live in the surroundings that you've got round here, power stations, muck stacks, with very little beauty? So when the rivers are awash with filth, the air is poisoned by industry and your house is black with grime, what's one more dropped cigarette packet? Just a drop in the ocean, isn't it? The problems should be worked at from both sides; first industry should show more responsibility and then small businesses.

It's no use putting a bin outside take-away food shops. People walk away eating their Chinese so perhaps the bins ought to be a few hundred yards up the road, otherwise we're going to get that used to seeing fish and chip suppers on the floor that people are going to stop taking notice. I'm sure if you start off with nice surroundings people respect that and keep it that way. It's all about education in the end.

□ I think a lot of people don't realise that every bag that's dropped ends up in a hedge bottom outside of town. I used to be like everybody else, not a litter lout, but indifferent. When I went to Switzerland I saw a five year old pick up some paper and tut tut at the adult that dropped it. When you see something like that it makes you think about your own attitudes. I'm much more caring now; if I have a drink of pop

in the car I leave the can inside and take it home, same with empty bags, I put them in my pocket.

□ One thing I can't bear to see is when people empty their car ashtrays straight out into the gutter. I had to go out into the street the other day with a dustpan and sweep up above forty tab ends.

□ You see a lot of scavenging birds at the side of the motorways these days, magpies and crows and that, living off sandwiches and stuff that gets thrown out of folks' cars. It's as though a whole new environment has grown up on motorway embankments. You see a lot of kestrels as well, they'll be after the mice that litter attracts.

Breaking out into the garden

□ I am a keen walker with my dogs and throughout our village everywhere I go I see the environment polluted. The hedge bottoms are a favourite place. Household refuse, discarded clothes, old mattresses, you name it and it's there. One favourite place is a disused railway cutting in Storr's Mill Wood. People come in their cars, and over the bridge it goes; the above mentioned stuff plus old TVs, car parts, carpets, fruiterers' rotted vegetables; what a disgusting sight this is. Everywhere I go I see cables stripped of their copper. Have a walk to the rear of Pye Avenue and you'll see what I mean. It doesn't matter where it goes as long as it's out of their way.

Monday morning through our village people patronising take-aways just discard the remains of Saturday or Sunday night's supper. There's beer cans and soft drink cans all over the place.

Then we have property developers and farmers who, where once stood healthy trees, a natural habitat for the birds and wildlife, just get their chainsaws or bulldozer in and down they come. Just to squeeze in a few more houses or to gain another yard of land, they take trees that have taken years to grow. As an example of this, there's a public footpath from Cows Lane to Darfield Road where once stood a lovely hawthorne, blackberry bushes and the occasional apple tree. Silkstone Construction moved in a few weeks ago with their heavy equipment and down the lot came, gone in a couple of hours. I protested to Barnsley MBC and the matter is in the hands of their Legal and Planning Department. Gone is the public footpath. Gone is the habitat for the birds and wildlife. I say the company should be made to restore the path and trees. What they can't do is put it back as it was. Councils have got to put a stop to this wholesale desecration of the countryside and the environment. Barnsley Council have got to use tree preservation orders. I once did that when I was a member at Cudworth.

□ When we were about nine and ten friends and I used to walk by a reservoir to a little valley called Marydale. A stream ran through the dale and reeds grew in the water. We used to paddle in the water and pick the blackberries in that season. The greatest treat was to collect reeds – we called them bullrushes – and make them into plaited whips and rattles. We plaited the reeds as we walked up the dale and through a wood called Scout Wood then onto the moors where we played in the grouse shooting butts. Then it was home for tea.

□ I remember coming home from school in the summertime, having tea which was always on the table as we came in, rushing through banana sandwiches, then trying my level best to get out of piano practice till later in the evening. If I was allowed to put it off for an hour or so I would run excitedly down through Birkwood Avenue, through somebody's garden, to be enthralled by the beauty and wonder of the bluebell wood. It's no longer there I'm afraid. This was on a steep slope and in bluebell time we spent

hours picking armfuls of huge bluebells which we took to school the next morning and put in 2lb jam jars on the window-sills.

□ My first experience out of the garden and into the world was when one by one we crept through the prickly hedge into the cow field taking care not to scratch ourselves or our clothes. The mother-die and buttercups were over the tops of our heads and we played hide and seek hidden from each other by the screen of tall grass. Suddenly there were loud shouts and a big man was towering above us. It was the farmer – we had seen him herding the cows through the street. "What the hell do you think you're doing?" It was the first time I'd heard the word hell outside of church. The terrible fear as we tried to get back through the hedge, scratching and tearing at our hands and clothes. "The mean old man," my mother said, "you weren't hurting anything." But it was a long time before we went there again.

The cow slaps on the streets always reminded me of that day.

□ We took about twenty kids tracking on the dell. I had no idea what tracking was so one of the kids organised it. He split the group into two teams and explained what they had to do. He went through the dell and hid two different sets of cards, one blue and one red. We had a red team and a blue team. The object of the tracking was for each team to find the ten cards of their colour. The first to find them won. The tracking lasted about two hours, something which was very tiring for the kids because the dell is on a very steep slope and they were going up and down it all the time looking for their cards. The pleasing thing about doing this tracking was that the kids had organised it themselves. There were no arguments, they just got on with enjoying the challenge. It just shows if kids' minds are occupied with something to do they stop being a problem. While they were tracking I videoed them and they even ignored that, which they hadn't done before.

On the way back we sat and watched people fishing in the ponds. Some of the kids who go fishing started telling the group of the size of fish they had caught. I don't know whether or not some of these stories were anglers' tales. We didn't really have time to look for wildlife so maybe the next time we can make a full day of it.

The best thing what came out of the day for me was to see them helping one another up and down the slope. If someone fell or slipped there were always one or two other kids rushing over to help them up and make sure they were okay.

□ Cudworth School Camp is a school camp and not a holiday camp as it is held in school time and is part of the school curriculum. It was set up after the idea was taken from Gordonstoun and aims to teach people initiative, friendliness and living together as well as independence. It was first organised in 1949 by the Cudworth Senior Boys' School and is held fifty miles away at Burnsall-in-Wharfedale.

Unfortunately the school, now the Cudworth Middle School, is due to close in July 1990 after being open for 55 years and so the school camp will come to an end after 42 years.

It has always been a great adventure and never more so than in 1949 when such an endeavour was quite new to this kind of education. The first camp was attended by thirty boys and three members of staff but after that I think the average number has been about fifty and sixty.

The early camps, in comparison with later ones, were quite primitive. For instance the sleeping tents were occupied by eight and sometimes ten boys who slept on the ground on straw palliasses, whereas in later camps the campers – now girls and boys – sleep five per tent on spring camp beds. The toilets are now individual chemical toilet tents, whereas the early camp toilets were open air with a screen round. The cooking arrangements

POST OFFICE
FOR
MONEY ORDER SAVINGS BANK
PARCEL POST
INSURANCE — ANNUITY BUSINESS

have also seen great changes. I'm not going to admit that the cooking changes are better but they are easier though perhaps less adventurous and I think less exciting. One cooking arrangement which has remained the same throughout the years is that one teacher and about six boys are responsible for the food for one day.

The early cooking was all done outside in the open air. Two long trenches were dug six feet long by nine inches wide and six inches deep. These were for the fires and all the cooking was done in this way in large iron dixies. If the weather was wet then the boys got wet because boys are often too lazy to put on weatherproofs. The teachers stayed dry because they had sense to use waterproofs.

Cooking today is done under cover in a large marquee. There is no kneeling because the cooking is done table high on cooking rings and even an oven, all run off calor gas. With open air cooking everything is much less predictable because it only needs the fireman to forget his fire for a short while and all goes off the boil and the meal is delayed. Or if the fireman is over enthusiastic, then the food gets burnt. All is eaten in the end because one rule of the camp is there is no grumbling.

One big change in the camps is the finance. Today with about fifty-odd campers the camp will cost in excess of three thousand pounds, whereas the first camp with thirty-three campers cost just over one hundred and fifteen pounds. One food item is very interesting; meat every day for the thirty-three campers for two weeks plus sausage for breakfast three times a week, resulted in a butcher's bill of seven pounds. Today the camps are quite self-supporting and cost each camper about sixty pounds for the two weeks in camp. The early camps cost each camper two pounds for the two weeks but to keep this cost down some money towards camp costs was raised by jumble sales and school concerts. Also some of the less affluent campers were helped by payments from the school funds.

In the forty-odd years of the camp much pleasure and excitement has been enjoyed by more than two thousand young campers and staff in one of the most beautiful parts of England.

□ I wonder why it is that events of the past seem to be more colourful and attractive when looked at through our present day eyes.

I am thinking particularly of events and activities in my childhood, such as our Sunday walks. These usually happened after teatime when the family, dressed in Sunday best garb, sallied forth after a lengthy discussion on where to go. Father it was who usually decided. My most favourite walk was to a popular beauty spot called Hallington Dene. It incorporated everything which made up fairyland; a bubbling stream, wild iris and bullrushes, leafy trees and bridges, culminating in a series of small brightly painted pagodas. This walk was a good two miles long and my short legs and Sunday shoes did nothing to detract from the pleasure of that outing.

I am told that today many of the trees have been removed – they were unsafe – but this is not such a bad thing because it is hoped the extra light will encourage the growth of the wild flowers we once knew such as the ragged robins, Star of Bethlehem, king cups and wild orchids. One day I shall return before my aged limbs protest.

□ Everyone has a favourite walk I'm sure. My favourite walk was where I lived when I was small from California, California near Barnsley that is, and into what was named Monkey Park. Why they named it that puzzles me because I never once saw a monkey.

Every Sunday my dad, brother, my dog and I would set off from Bloomhouse Lane and past the little tin bungalows to the crossroads and walk straight on to Warren

Away in a Manger

Lane. When I was a child I spent many happy times rolling down the hill and jumping over the stones. At the right-hand side were lovely green fields with a stile. This was where we would sit and have a little rest. There I would make daisy rings threading each daisy through each stalk and place it round my dog's neck. She was ever so patient, she wouldn't try and get out of it, she was as happy as I was.

Back to the left side were a few large houses. One of them always enchanted me, it was a large Tudor house which stood in its own grounds, a long winding path led up to the house. I always remember asking my dad everytime we passed, "Is that house haunted?" He would say, "Dunt bi daft lass tha's noa such things us spirits." I realise now he was only kidding me, I know different. I would stand outside the grounds for what seemed ages, just admiring some of the lovely flowers and large trees.

When my dad could finally drag me away we would carry on walking down the lane where one road to the left would lead you to Woolley Village. We would walk down past there and take a cut off to the right until we came to Sandy Lane. At each side of the lane were wild flowers with cornfields at each side, the smell was lovely and the lane was soft under foot, hence the name, Sandy Lane. This led you on to Wakefield Road. This was a main road but there was no fear of being run over, there wasn't that many cars.

We would carry on for what seemed to be ages until we came to another field which we would cross and come to a farm, carry straight on and cross the stile and down into Monkey Park, where there was a row of little old houses and fields at the other side of the lane. At the end of the lane was my grandma's house where she would be waiting for us with a welcoming smell of fresh baked bread.

I have moved to a different village now and have only passed in the car but it looks so different. The tiny tin bungalows have gone and been replaced by brick ones, the plantings look burnt and parts of it fenced off. There are more houses on Warren Lane and the Tudor house doesn't seem as intriguing as it did when I was small, although it still looks secluded and haunted. Sandy Lane looks overgrown and spoilt by no-one caring for it. Now there are no wild flowers just nettles. Wakefield Road traffic travels past every second, you wouldn't feel safe walking on this stretch anymore. Fumes from the cars pollute the air and houses have replaced the empty green fields although there does seem to be a crossing down into Monkey Park. All the houses have gone and been replaced by two garages. Nothing looks or smells the same; the grass looks dull not a fresh green as it did before. It makes me sad because when I have grandchildren I will never be able to make them believe what things were like about 35 years ago.

□ At the top of Hunningley Lane were potato fields with pointed topped walls. We attempted to walk on these walls to and from school with many a tumble and grazed knees. Now there is a housing estate on these fields but the cemetery next to it has been left undisturbed as it should be. The house adjoining, an old stone one, has been boarded up and a new modern bungalow built for the caretaker. The cornfield is still there but the hedgerow has altered. When I remember the road was wider and there was a steep banking to the cornfield. Some of the tumbledown stone walls have been left. The banking on the left of the road is about fifeen feet high.

Originally on the right side was an old farm, now demolished and more private houses built. The garage on the corner is still there and beyond the private houses was White Cross Wood. We spent many happy hours there as children but it is altered for a newer generation. In my younger days there were no trees, just big holes where they had been uprooted before the war. Now the area has been landscaped into playing fields and a football ground. Yes, the younger generations will benefit but I wonder who had the most fun!

□ I stood waiting for the bus into Barnsley. It was a grey day, the air was thick with sulphur fumes. I could even taste it. Just a little way up the hill was Royston Drift Mine, opposite it was the Coking Plant. Thinking back, I never thought about them; when you are brought up in a place you do not notice the environment, it is just there. I had lived away for twenty-five years and had come back to Royston.

The bus came and I thought about my young days when I took this journey every day to work in Barnsley. It was Wednesday market day, and as the bus pulled into the station the noise was horrific, all the buses seemed to be blowing their horns. As I watched I realised it was to warn people that they were backing out from the stands, a crazy procedure. All the passengers were packed down one side of the station just like cattle in pens.

Was this our new bus station – who had designed it? Who sanctioned it to be built? Twenty-five years earlier we had had a good station complete with toilets and waiting room. As I came out of the station the first thing I saw was a large concrete office block with a concrete box stuck on top of it. No open market stalls now, just a large concrete multi-storey car park, beside it a concrete market hall; ugly, depressing, grey, its only redeeming feature is it kept the rain off you.

The feel of the old Barnsley had gone. Some of the old buildings are still there and they are the nicest part of the town now.

I thought about my mother's house in East End Crescent in Royston. They had just been modernised with a huge housing grant. The kitchens had been extended and built with some kind of plywood – incredible but true! In winter when the steam from cooking and washing got on the walls it froze the wood and it was like standing in an ice box; as fast as the walls were painted, black mould grew on the walls. Who designed and sanctioned them?

Now sixteen years later we are to have a new shopping complex in Barnsley, it is to be built on the old Alhambra Cinema site and is to be called the Alhambra. I hope the planners have got it right this time. This is our environment and any change had better be for the better. It makes a big difference to our lives; it affects the way we think and the way we feel.

□ I have always loved trees and I was very pleased when we moved into our new house and there was this lovely mature silver birch tree at the bottom of our garden. Actually it belonged to the people next door but I think trees are our heritage and belong to everyone. Its branches spread gracefully over our fence giving us privacy and also shelter on rare hot days. It gave me immense pleasure as I only come to life in the spring, and I used to love to watch the buds appear and then give birth to a cascade of catkins. I used to think that there was nothing to compare with this in terms of beauty. I also loved to watch all kinds of different birds busily making their nests. There was lots of activity around this tree.

You can imagine how I felt when my husband awoke me one morning, and said that the tree had disappeared. I shot out of bed as quickly as if someone had shouted "Fire!" and looked through the bedroom window. Sure enough the tree had gone. There were no traces of any branches lying around. All that was left was a great ugly stump. I was very upset.

Later that morning, it became obvious that my neighbour was the perpetrator as I saw him tidying the tree up. Trying hard to control my anger I went out and confronted him about this dastardly act. All he had to say was that it wanted to come down. I had visions of him having a conversation with it, the tree pleading to

Steve McClarence

be chopped in half. I told him I was very disappointed and walked quickly away not wanting to show my true feelings.

Throughout the day it was my favourite topic, as I went on and on about it, and the rain forests being chopped down, and the harm it was doing to the environment. I felt as if New Lodge had suffered a great ecological imbalance.

After a while I think my husband was getting quite fed up with me although he did sympathise and offer some information about silver birch trees being a protected species. It was not much help to me at this time.

A few days later hundreds of small red roses that used to peep through our trellis also disappeared. It reminded me of a book I read about Joan Crawford, she used to chop rose trees down in the middle of the night.

I could just picture my neighbours rising in the small hours with their hatchets ready for their next assault on nature. It was as if everything of beauty was being removed.

Strangely enough, a few days later I was given two beautiful shrubs, and two large climbing roses which we planted in the empty spaces. Along with our young silver birch trees our garden will bloom once again.

I really felt that God had restored the balance of nature that day.

□ It happened in the woodwork room at the Cudworth Modern School. One boy, who shall be nameless, repeatedly spoilt his piece of work. After several disasters I said to him, "Look John I can't keep giving you pieces of wood to spoil – do you think wood grows on trees?"

"No Sir," he replied.

□ In the 1930s I always thought Cudworth was unique because there could have been few, if any, other villages with a golf course on its border. It was a nine-hole course and I think it opened in the late 1920s. It was never a prosperous club but it was a very friendly one and you never saw anyone playing on their own.

There was no entrance fee to join the club and the annual membership fee was just £2 but even so some members found this fee difficult to find at the beginning of each year. Caddies by the way were paid threepence per round.

I never remember the club having more than about fifty members, and three-quarters of these came from Cudworth while the remainder came from Barnsley, Royston, Shafton and Grimethorpe.

The club held a licence but as it could not afford a steward, the bar was help-yourself-and-please-put-the-money-in-the-till. This system always worked very well.

One member told me a story about him being a shift worker on the railway and often when he played during the day he was the only member on the course. In order to have a partner he took his four year old son to play against. The son had a small set of golf clubs which his father had made, and for a four year old he was a useful little golfer. He played his son giving the boy five strokes a hole, they played for a bar of chocolate and if the little boy did not win the sweets he cried all the way home.

The club closed in 1941 because in 1940 many of the young members, including myself, were called up for service in the armed forces and the few members left found it impossible to carry on with the much reduced income.

During the war the course was put under the plough and it was never possible after the war to re-open the Cudworth Golf Club.

□ As children we always went down Carlton fields to play. We jumped across a small wooden bridge and then went along under the bridge to the canal. We would jump across the shute where the coal would go down.

In the summer holidays we would take bread and jam and a bottle of pop and go down to Storr's Mill Wood. We would

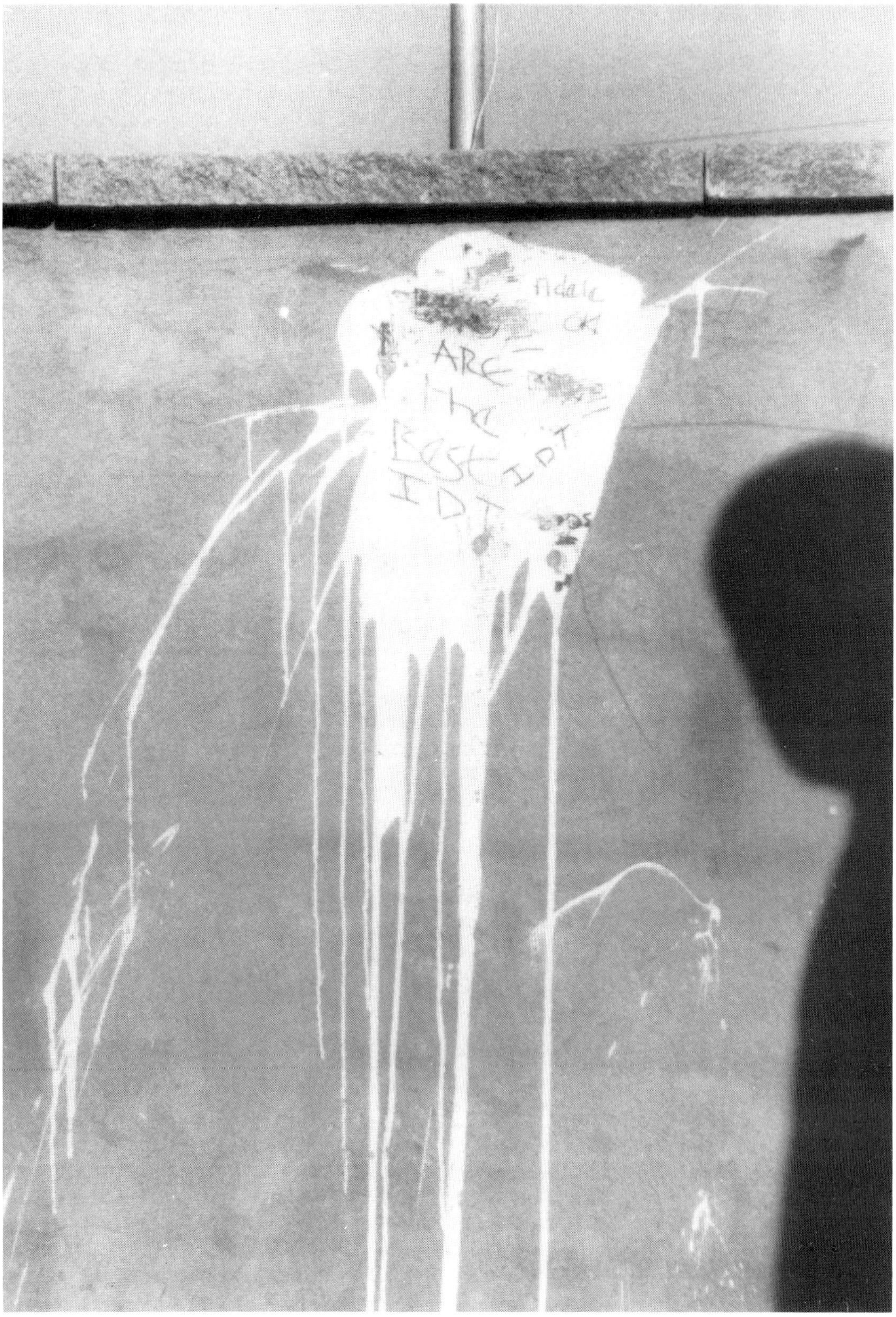

Steve McClarence

In the shade

paddle in the stream. We played for hours in Cudworth Park.

□ We used to go to that canal to watch a beautiful blonde woman diving in to swim. I won't mention her name but she was very popular among the lads who hid behind the trees watching her because she swam naked.

□ When children were young in the Twenties and Thirties, one of the pastimes was walking. We went along Lunn Road, past the well that was situated at the bottom of Wells Street, past Silverwood's Farm, down Carr Lane towards the wood, which used to be full of bluebells, crossed a stream that was spanned by a rockerty wooden bridge, on to Silverwood's Ring Farm then on to the rifle range.

We had a carrier bag with jam sandwiches and a bottle of water with lemonade crystals. We spent lovely afternoons there and before leaving for home we picked bluebells which had to be put in a jam jar and left on the windowsill. It was supposed to be bad luck to take them indoors.

□ After chapel on Sunday evening, we would walk over the fields to Brierley down the Blackety, across one field over the seventy-seven steps, through another field, then passing the sewage farm and up the lane onto Brierley Road and back down to Shafton. I recently took the same walk to find the seveny-seven steps had vanished and the sewage works was now derelict. There one could get loads of blackberries for making jam. Not many people make jam today.

When I was a child before the NHS, once a year we had a hospital sing in Shafton Park. The choir sang from the cricket pavilion steps. A collection was taken and the proceeds given to Barnsley Beckett Hospital, which is no longer there.

Another walk to Felkirk Church over the the fields is almost the same today apart from another set of seventy-seven steps which have been taken down. The steps in both places went over the railway lines which are no longer in use. One line went from Goldthorpe to Wakefield and the other from Monckton pit to join up with the Wakefield line. The train running on this line was called either the Little Billy or The Titanic and even during the war when my friend was working at Pinderfields Hospital, she used to travel on this train. If the driver was in a good mood he would drop her off at the bottom of their orchard where she could walk home. It was rather strange that the tree nearest the railway line was the first to be stripped.

□ One of my special secret places used to be at the bottom of my grandparents' garden at Sidcop (Cudworth). It was a clearing in a clump of bushes where I used to go after Sunday dinner.

I'd sit in the middle of these bushes all afternoon thinking no-one could find me there. I'd take mental notes of the people who passed by on the back lane.

People like Geronimo or Sitting Bull would ride past with their tribes and, after they'd gone by I'd run to the outhouse which used to be the fort, and I'd inform the General of the U.S. Cavalry of the oncoming attack by the savage redskins!

□ I remember going down to the Storr's Mill Wood during the school holidays with my family and other families in the street. We took sandwiches and pop for a picnic and got pure water from a spring in the wood.

We used to go down Carlton fields on Sunny Bank which was a slope leading down to the swamps. In summer we used to roll down and in winter we used a sledge. Then in summer we all went round the hedgerows with jam jars collecting blackberries.

□ It was years since I had been back to the village. I felt a bit uncomfortable at the car boot sale. Not that I have anything against them but I couldn't help thinking it

Steve McClarence

The Shadow of the NCB

was a bit unseemly to be holding them on Sunday mornings on the site where the village chapel had once stood. It was a warm day, the smell of hot-dogs mingled with those of greasy chips and vinegar. I wondered what our old Sunday School Superintendent, Henry Clark, would have said. He'd preached damnation so many times to us as children if we abused the Sabbath. I shrugged the feeling off.

Alex had seen what he wanted straight away, a fishing line. He paid 75p for it. Once it was in his grasp, he couldn't wait to dangle it in the water.

"OK Alex, how about you and me going to the river where I used to play?"

"Great, Grandma!" Alex said. He picked up half a hot-dog that someone had thrown away. "This'll do for bait," and he grabbed at a plastic bag that was drifting past his feet and put his bait in it.

His hand in mine we set off to the river that was ten minutes walk away. I'd lived in the village more than the first half of my life. Now I had to stand and get my bearings before crossing the road. The motorway had divided the village. There were two roads instead of one and the motorway junction. The river had been diverted, the bridge over it had disappeared. So had the old ash tree that had served as our bus stop and shelter for so many years. We crossed the road and entered the old part of the village.

Familiar cottages had been tastefully renovated to keep their old world look. Gardens that had once been worked as vegetable patches were now lawned and flower filled. Expensive climbers trailed over house walls and over boundaries, where once honeysuckle and dog rose spilled over broken walls onto uneven paths.

"They've made a good job of this road, Alex," I said gratefully. "It used to be full of potholes." We passed through the gate that led into the field by the river.

"There's the island, look, and I'll show you where your dad and Uncle John used to fish when they were boys."

"Will there be any fish left do you think, Grandma? What kind were they?"

"Oh, sticklebacks and minnows. Tiddlers really." He ran on ahead of me making a path for us both in the long grass.

The island, still starred with daisies, was smaller than I remembered, washed away by time and weather. The large stepping stones that led to the island were coated in long strands of moss. The stones were part of the river now. Not ours. Not for us.

I took Alex round the bend of the river where the water ran slower, deeper, almost still.

"Was it here Grandma, I bet it was here", Alex shouted.

"Ssh, that's right. Here's where they used to be. Now you get on with your fishing and I'll sit and rest."

Happily he baited his line and cast it. We both sat still, he keeping his eyes on his steady line and me swatting at midges that hovered round my head.

Over on the other bank, families were shuffling past on the start of a nature trail. They walked between a fenced path that took them to parklands. I thought how orderly they walked, rather like cows at milking time, the restricting fences keeping them at a steady pace, and away from the grass. I recalled summers past, when this part of the river was host to parties of school children. They came on Sunday School outings and ran races for monkey nuts and oranges. They paddled in the river and swung out over the water hanging on to an old rope slung over branches in the tall trees. The children came from far sounding places, Redbrook, Wilthorpe, Gawber, Barnsley. Our world was so small then.

"Grandma I've caught one and oh! it's a big one. Look at it jerking the line. Give me a hand quick." Laughing we wound the line in.

"I bet it's an old boot, Alex."

"No. It's struggling, look." At the end of the line was a plump trout. Silver grey with a soft pink belly.

Alex's face was streaked with sweat. We managed to get the fish off the hook. It lay gasping. Alex hit it on the head with a stone and I wrapped it in dock leaves, put it in the plastic bag and then into my shopping bag.

"I wonder what they'll say to it at home. Can I have another go, Grandma?" he begged.

"Go on then," I said. We settled down again.

A loud voice calling from over the field disturbed us. "What the blazes do you think you're doing there?" An angry red-faced man in his shirt sleeves came running over to us.

"I'm resting while my grandson tries his new line out. He bought it this morning," I explained. "Why, what's the matter?"

"You're trespassing. That's what's the matter." He glared from me to Alex who had just pulled his empty line out of the water. "Can't you read! It says no trespassing plain enough on the gate you've come through," he said angrily.

"Look I'm sorry," I apologised. "But it's years since I was here. I was looking for the island and this bend of the river. I was so pleased to see everything as I remembered it and I didn't notice any sign."

"Well, no damage done I expect," and he looked again at Alex's disappointed face and at the empty line. "But you'll have to be off. I don't want anybody on my land. I've some prime fish in my part of the river."

"Come on Alex," I said and picked up my bag. Alex wound his line up and we set off back.

We passed the island and the moss covered stones for the last time. I thought how lucky I had been as a child to feel them warm from the sun under my bare feet. I looked back over the field where Alex and I had cut our path that morning, and remembered when paths were once well trodden and the river was for us all.

Alex pulled at my sleeve, "You never told him about the fish, Grandma."

"He never asked," and I winked at him, happy that we'd managed to share a perfect moment in what was now a secret place.

NEW BOOKS
FROM YORKSHIRE ART CIRCUS

NO TIME FOR DYING
Joan Thornton £6.50

ISBN 0 947780 49 1

What do you want to do when you retire? This book is an inspiration for anyone who thinks that life is over when you reach 65. Yorkshire people talk about taking up windsurfing, gold prospecting and travelling the world. Others look back on treasured memories or reveal how they cope with the money and health worries that come with growing older. Nostalgia, wisdom, humour — these anecdotes speak with the richness of experience. A book to have at your bedside whether you're 25 or 95!

YORKSHIRE MIXTURE
Edited by Joan Thornton £4.99

ISBN 0 947780 62 9

A diverting collection of 24 new short stories, all with a Yorkshire flavour. Who can resist a story which starts "Crabs. Hundreds of them. They've escaped from his motorbike. They're running riot. He's mad." If you enjoy suspense, humour and macabre twists of plot packed into short tales, this is the book for you.